Edmond Richmond Allyn

The overcoming Kingdom

Edmond Richmond Allyn
The overcoming Kingdom
ISBN/EAN: 9783337171490

Printed in Europe, USA, Canada, Australia, Japan

Cover: Foto ©ninafisch / pixelio.de

More available books at **www.hansebooks.com**

THE
OVERCOMING KINGDOM

BY
MICHAEL.

IN SEVEN LECTURES ON THE
BOOK OF REVELATIONS.

And He shall rule them with a Rod of Iron; as the vessels of a Potter, shall they be broken to shivers, even as I received of my Father.—Rev. 2:27.

Harrison, So. Dak.
March, 1899.

Entered according to act of Congress
in the year 1899, by
REV. E. R. ALLYN,
In the office of the Librarian of Congress,
at Washington.

The Foundation Uncovered.

LECTURE FIRST.

As the author of these lectures grasps his pen to try to unfold to his fellow man, the mysteries of the Book of Revelations, he is aware of the responsibility he assumes before an enlightened age. Were it not for a keen impressive sense of duty, the work would be left to abler hands than his own. He courteously asks the considerate attention, rather than the criticism and censure of his readers.

Before proceeding to consider the Book in course, distinct from its connection with other books of the Bible, we call attention to its importance as the last of the inspired revelations given to man. Its scenes and visions are of transcendant importance, to this age and condition of the world.

Its revelations are given on the hipothesis that the foundation and beginning of a Divine Empire had been established in the typical city of Jereusalem, which was to obtain universal local organized bodies under the ministry of the various gifts of the Spirit. In order to preserve to man his right to life in the new earth and bring his estate into it; into these local bodies, and under spiritual ministry and control, joint heirship is made the basic principle in the new earth to permit mans spiritual cooperation in all that relates to the new empire.

It will occur to us, just here, that any rule or empire is responsible for the effect any form of civilization may have upon its subjects; therefore it is absolutely necessary that a spiritual administration should produce a new civilization, that would in every way conserve the mind and work of the Spirit; and relieve its subjects from the effect of a mingling with all other forms, while building up that form which is spiritual and perfect and will stand forever.

To give a forecast of the fortunes the new kingdom in its peaceful conflict with the corrupt sceptres of universal rule, and to lay broad and deep, in the inspired record for the comfort of the faithful, the assurance of its triumph in the earth, its now corronated King appears in vision to one of the Twelve Founders, who under the guidance and mighty sanctions of the Holy Ghost, had planted his sceptre and disclosed the eternal foundation of His Empire, in the typical city of Jerusalem in the year A D. 33.

HIS MESSAGE TO HIS SUBJECTS.

To seven organized bodies of His people, He delivers a message showing His close and constant inspection of their state and work, under His spiritual ministration.

He appears to the Revelator as the "First and the last." (first in creation last in redemption.) The first begotten from the dead, "THE PRINCE OF THE KINGS OF THE EARTH."

His majesty distinguishes him as a victor, able to fulfill His promises, and execute his threatenings.. We may apply the lesson briefly. Loyalty is the condition of heirship. We suggest that the number seven, is indicative of completeness here, as in other places, and in this instance covers the ground of danger, and extent of reward.

One of the rewards offered was that He would give them power over the nations, and they should rule them with a rod of iron. That as the vessels of a potter, should they be broken into shivers, even as He received His Father.

If the domain of any nation was interspersed with local bodies vested with primitive gifts of the Spirit, and cooperating under joint heirship, in building their own civilization and maintaining their own institutions, and leaving out evil agencies which the world tolerates; that nation, it might be said was shivered.

However much we may admire human rule, it never can deliver man from his mightiest foes of suffering disease, and death, nor from being exposed to poverty, nor from being the victim of coveteousness and greed. Among all forms of rule there is but one that is pure and great.

The author will here meet the objection that the position assumed is materialistic, by replying that any finished work by spiritual agencies is perfect, and that God's work is perfect and complete in any part of His creation.

We are living eighteen centuries nearer the time when every eye shall see Him, and all the kindreds of the earth shall wail because of Him, than when this Revelation was written; and time the great producer and disposer of events is leaving its record for our admonition.

From our standpoint, many things relating to the Kingdom have had their fulfillment and their work has relegated their claims to the past. We may note the rise and reign of anti-Christ and the breaking of its power to consume it to the end. The man of sin must be revealed and we have had, and doubtless are having his revelation. Both the world and the church must learn the great lesson, that without the Christ His people can do nothing; and that He walks in the midst of the Seven Golden Candle Sticks both to admonish and reward them. Anti Christ took time to acquire dominion or supremacy, to effect complete cooperation with the scarlet colored beast of John's vision. So we must give the Kingdom of Christ time to emerge from its wilderness of obscurity, and afflicted state.

We note that the Kingdom must have had its introduction to the world or there could have been no opposition of opposing powers, that could have been designated anti Christ. But the light Christ gave the world is fast dispelling the darkness, produced by his fading power, and the end of his sway is approaching. "When the Kingdom and Dominion, and the greatness of the Kingdom under the whole Heaven, shall be given to the people of the saints of the most high, and all dominions shall serve and obey Him."—Dan. 7:27.

The time seems long, and the overcoming Kingdom ought to be here. The bride ought to be making herself ready. The mass of mankind seems to have a vague uncertainty as to what it is, and how to find it. But it is to be presumed that all uncertainty will vanish before its sceptre when its power again challenges an enlightened age.

It does not seem presumption to say that what it was at its founding, it is now. The Kingdom is the body of Christ and cannot change unless He changes.

He never set up any spurious church and called it his Kingdom, nor would the righteous God have approved it with the gift of His spirit.

When the sceptre finds subjects who have light and faith enough to come clearly under its sway, and within its conditions, the cooperation of the corronated Christ will not be wanting. It never failed to fill his covenant and never will, as long as there is a soul it can redeem. It must be now what it was at its founding, or it perished in the wilderness, where it was nourished for a time, times, and a half, from the face of the serpent. But it was reinforced by a host of overcoming heirs, who loved not their lives even unto death, and who will share the reign of the saints. The Kingdom had its purpose and must have its essentials, that constitute its potency and pomer, and if they are wanting the work of building His empire cannot go on. If a false light is exhibited he removes the candlestick.

Let us look at its founding and examine its foundation; time A. D. 33; place Jerusalem, the city of the great kings; occasion, Pentecost, a feast of weeks; attendants, representatives of all nations under the heaven; authorities, twelve living witnesses of His life, ministry, doctrine, miracles, death, resurection and ascention, chosen before, and instructed for their work. For the purpose of conveying divine authority the Holy Ghost came with the sound of a rushing mighty wind and filled the place where they were sitting: They were filled with the spirit. Cloven tongues like as of fire sat upon each of them, and they delivered the Proclamation of His Kingdom in the language of all the different nations present.

Two distinct agencies in distinct departments of His kingdom, belong to the advent of the spirit, in its work through the Apostolic commission.

The first work was to proclaim the corronation of Christ, the terms or process of adoption and the gift of the spirit.

The second work to be done, was to establish in the earth the divine order, unity, and cooperation of the adopted subjects of His kingdom under the guidance and ministry of the Spirit.

The first conveys His authority, and witness of the Spirit to the world.

The second establishes the relation of sonship, brotherhood, unity, cooperation, and the righteous character of the citizenship in His kingdom.

A failure to recognize these two distinct offices of the divine authority, leaves us entirely on the sea of congecture, as to what constitutes the complete foundation of apostles and prophets, with Christ as its chief corner stone.

One fact ought to impress all minds with the sense of the highest responsibility here; and that is that the kingdom thus founded was vested with overcoming power, and it was this power that stamped the sceptre of Christ with both the divinity and humanity of his nature, and justified all that was done to create a like harmony in the relations of His body.

Before leaving the foundation let us examine the building which has been "Builded together for a habitation of God through the Spirit," and prepared to "grow into a holy temple in the Lord."

All that believed were together. They had all obeyed the same law of adoption, and received the same spirit. They were of one heart, and of one soul They enjoyed earth's blessings in gladness of heart; none said that ought of the things he possesed were his own.

They brought their possessions with them and turned all over to the disposition of divine authority.

They continued steadfastly in the apostles doctrine; fellowship breaking bread and prayers. We have in this foundation all that is required to the founding of a new and spiritual empire, and if we invoke its guidance and agency in serving our king we must take on such relations to the purpose, nature and work of the sceptre, as will bring ourselves and our work and our powers into covenrnt relation with our Lord.

The authority here revealed and work done, cannot be disregarded by nations or individuals. It is God's work and cannot be repealed, changed or disobeyed. It would involve disloyalty to the King. Time, place, events, with the awful sanctions which accompany its advent, all distinguish it as the sceptre over all nations.

What it demanded was obeyed then and must be now. God enfored it with his judgements then, and will enforce it as long as it has a foe left.

That sceptre demanded its sway in all things in the hearts, lives and works of all men. It convinced and convicted men that Christ was Lord of all. It demanded repentance and they repented. It demanded baptism and thousands were baptised. It demanded separation in order to unity and cooperation, and all that believed were together. It demanded unity of soul and purpose and all were of one heart, and of one soul. It demanded cessation of the right to individual monopoly of earthly possessions and all that had them sold them and laid the money at the apostles feet. It demanded renunciation of human selfishness and none said that ought of the things he possessed were his own.

It demanded steadfast allegiance, and they continued steadfast in the apostles teaching.

They were promised the gift of the Holy Ghost and they received it. They were promised the presence of the King by His Spirit and they had it.

Here then, is the living foundation of the living kingdom of the living Christ. It harmonizes with Himself, with all He had taught, with all that He had done, with all that He had prayed for. It fulfilled God's promise, Jesus' mission, man's need, and Satan's overthrow. It will overturn Babylon, renew the earth and stand forever. For its rejection Jerusalem was destroyed and the nation of the Jews wiped out as a nation; for disobeying it Annanias and Sappira were stricken dead. All elements in nature obeyed its King. Prophets searched diligently for its coming glory, and none but Satan and corrupt earthly powers, drunken with greed and the love of vain glory will be angry at its triumph.

Both the prophecies and promises indicate that power was to attend the subjects of the divine kingdom in the work and conflict of its conquest.

Our Lord gave the seventy, power over unclean spirits, to heal the sick, cleanse the lepers and raise the dead; and when they reported to Him that even devils were subject to them through His name, He said; "I beheld Satan as lightning fall from heaven." A bold acclamation of a conquerer, because His subjects clothed with power could dethrone the Devil. If the sceptre of Christ can undo what Saton does, then Satan is vanquished and his kingdom falls. "I walk in the midst of the seven golden candle sticks, an ever living Christ in the midst of an ever living kingdom." We suggest that Christ intended that in his kingdom the world should find salvation for soul and body. Healing of body, healing of mind, and access to the Tree of Life, which is for the healing of the nations.

Let us pause a moment and reflect. Jesus Christ and a loving subject of his kingdom, both one, and the suffering member of his body, cannot have the healing virtues of the Great Physician, when attacked by pain and suffering, from an inherited weakness of body. Faith in Jesus must say he can. Unbelief, even in the church doubtless would say no. But thank God the unbelief of an unbeliever, cannot reach either the power or willingness of the living Christ.

In sincerity and charity we ask, was not the kingdom of our Lord set up under the dispensation of the Holy Spirit? And must it not remain under that dispensation until it is displaced by one more potent?

Does the agency of the mighty and eternal spirit, of the living God, leave a redeemed man or woman, to the sole dependance on human skill, and the agency of poisonous drugs, to prolong a life that may be of more value to God and man than all the pride and skill of human bias? If the kingdom of our blessed Lord has in it any power of recovery and restitution for our suffering, corrupted, enlightened age, in His name let us bring it into relief.

One visitation of His divine witness to our loyalty and conformity to the divine will and purpose of our Lord, is worth a thousand con- ctures, opinions, theories or professions.

The voice is sounding in our ear today: "Fear not little flock, it is your Father's good pleasure to give you the kingdom." The reality and depth of that pleasure is unquestioned, but where is the flock whose complete possession of the sceptre, bears witness to the giving.

Does it not seem clear to us that when Christ fails to clothe His people with the very substance of His promises, that He would be with them to the end; without the cooperation of His spiritual power, His sceptre in the hands of men is weaker than that of his foes?

It is clear that if our Lord by the finger of God could cast out devils, the kingdom has come to us, but why have we not its primitive witness that it has come? The author knows of no reason, but that we are not maintaining its distinctive order, and cannot show to a corrupt age the beauty, purity and power of its divine civilization.

The Overcoming Kingdom must be heralded by its own Divine Proclamation.

I tremble when I read Paul:

"Though we, or an angel from heaven, preach any other gospel than that we have preached unto you let him be accursed. For I never received it from man neither was I taught it but by revelation of Jesus Christ."

There can be no danger greater, or mistake more fatal, than for an empire to authorize or send out, an unqualified or false embassador; and it is our glory and safety, that God has kept his own record of the founding of the kingdom of His Son, and that it stands squarely on its own divine foundation.

But it is no wonder that God does not bear witness to all the false, conflicting, contradictory reports, the oposition has received about it and the nature of its authority. Even its friends have in their zeal mutilated the divine standard, until neither the world nor ourselves are able to recognize it, from their report of it. Opinion, philosophy, theory, feeling, experience and even success and failure, have all been employed as its witnesses.

If the Proclamation of Emancipation issued by the martyred Lincoln, had been treated by this nation as the church and the world has treated the divine proclamation of the Prince of the Kings of the Earth, the black race might still have been in slavery. Though we cannot exactly define what effect such a mistake might have had upon our nation; it is easy to see and clear to understand what effect the mutilation of the authority of Christ has had upon the spirituality, unity, cooperation, and civilization of the empire of the corronated Christ.

Where then does the kingdom of Christ get its proclamation? From the kingdom itself. Repeat the authority of the King in all it commanded, in all it promised, in all it done. Proclaim the kingdom in all its completeness and order. It is His proclamation to all nations; why leave out anything pertaining to it? If we think it contains too much dare we modify it? It is a divine foundation. Will we take any of the stones out of it? It is perfect. Will we mar it? If we do we intercept its purpose, forfeit its promises, incur the displeasure of the King and mislead our fellow men.

The writer has long stifled the conviction that the kingdom of Christ was itself a complete Christian cooperation, and that all of its work, institutions, and achievements, should be sanctified by His will and be carried on in His name. But today disclaims any faith in corrupt earthly power to establish, conduct, or furnish such cooperation, or to exhibit its pure civilization. It is not their province and wholly beyond their power.

The extreme individualism of this nineteenth century civilization, never did obtain in any rule to which God gave his sanction. Its assumption of right is antagonistic to the equilibrium of a rule for all. It is a breeder of covetousness and selfishness and its power of self laudation, unfits man to love his neighbor as himself, much less to esteem his brother, more highly than himself. It is a promoter of dishonesty, injustice and crime. Principle, conscience and purity are all sacrificed on its alter; and the road to wealth and distinction is paved with skeletons that might have reflected the image of Christ. The power of self control must be regained by man before he is fit to be an empire in himself or is made a king and priest unto God in things that are perfect.

The dependance of the church for its industrial opportunities and social standards, has helped amazingly to whitewash a corrupt civilization, and to a greater extent has clothed it with the livery of heaven in the popular mind. From the standpoint of prudence and spiritual economy, have a geographical instead of an invisible line. Demonstrate that there is one institution that can exist without the saloon, the gambling den, the variety theater, the sweat shop, the secret clan, or even the poisonous viands of a world's patented drugs.

The world is ripe for an institution that can discern between the good and the bad, between the useful and the needless, between economy and worthless extravagance, between comfort and security, and mere pompous vanity and display. The divine kingdom has the right poise before an enlightened age, but it is not the religio-world mixture of today. If the kingdom of Christ is not constructed to acquire domain, how will he attain possession of the uttermost parts of the earth?

One of God's covenant promises to Isreal was that if they maintained their separateness, He would abundantly bless them in their temporal affairs. Without considering its typical application, we enquire, why not give His Son the benefit of this opportunity to bless His kingdom, without directly building up Babylon, and aiding the Devil with his seductive institutions?

We would rather see one single county consecrated to Christ, than vote the prohibition ticket or any other ticket, or than send a religious petition to congress. It is a piteous sight to see whole regiments of the heirs of high heaven bending low before corrupt law and custom, and beseeching Satan to draw back his hidra head, when Christ by a divine constitution has given them the power through cooperation, to shut him and his agencies out of their domain and communion.

I must protest Christ never intended His subjects should serve these invasions in pursuit of home or bread; but by seeking first His kingdom and its righteousness they would inherit all they needed.

Before God destroyed the Antideluveans He got Noah into the ark. Before he destroyed Sodom He sent Lot out of it. Before He punished the Egyptians He got the Israelites beyond their border. Before literal Babylon was overthrown He took the Children of Israel back to their Canaan, and before mystical Babylon falls His people must come out of her to be saved from her sins and plagues We suggest the New Jerusalem ought to be the proper place for them to come.

Do we ever think how exhaustive of our strength, physical and moral, this diversion from pure spiritual ends and aims of the toil wealth, spiritual influence and power, this indiscriminate mingling becomes. Is there nothing better than this for a redeemed race?

Just prior to the time Jesus gave His message to the churches, He gave a clear demonstration of His authority to the nations. The import of the event of Israel's overthrow is that the stone their builders rejected, had become the head of the corner and that all power in heaven and earth had been given him.

The Jews as a nation rejected the authority of the Christ over all nations, and the fate of that nation stands today as a signal warning to all nations, of the folly of building on any other foundation than the authority of the corronated Christ.

Have we carefully noted the reason why they stumbled? Certainly it was their untastefulness for the loveliness, and meekness, and purity of His character, and that of his sceptre. But to us the reproof comes with equal force. With a glimpse at Him our affinity for the rule or custom that accords the same right to evil agencies, as it does to justice and purity, must weaken. Had the sceptre contained less it would have misrepresented Christ, for before His corronation He had proclaimed and enforced upon His followers all it contained. "He that forsaketh not all that he hath cannot be my disciple." Now hardly (with what difficulty) shall they that have riches enter the kingdom of heaven. Customs change conditions. Today they would be accorded the right to come in and keep their millions and flattered to keep them in.

It is enough for the servant that he be as his Lord. We need to think of His humbling

Himself and becoming obedient—even to the death of the cross. Think of the riches He exchanged for poverty, that we through His poverty might become rich.

And then seek to evade the very means and measures He has employed to secure our exaltation with Him in His kingdom. The highest province of the wealth of this world, is its use for the good of all. Its diversion from this high purpose, its misappropriation to needless and bad ends is wrong, and that Christ relieved His people of the temptation which unrestrained human ambition always has incured, is a wise provision and a blessing.

That which responds to the energy and industry of man, may become a mighty agent and factor in his spiritual recovery from the law of sin and death, or it may act like an immense weight upon his nature to hold hold him in carnalty and servitude, to a love which is the root of all evil.

We may contrast the wisdom of a law of joint heirship under spiritual administration, with the principle of unrestrained natural right, with the scope it gives to an unholy ambition, and find in the latter our world's long record of strife, war, subugation, slavery, murder, crime, degredation and suffering. In the former we have an infalible arbitrer. All questions of right are constitutionally settled. The abundance of all is far greater and more available, than that which is consumed in the smoke of battle, swallowed in the thirst for liquid fire, or lavished on the alter of human law, in the fruitless task of administering justice. In prophetic vision we may look forward on the sea of human strife when this iron rule of the divine sceptre has banished envy and discord, when nations learn war no more, and when swords become plow shares, and spears are made pruning hooks, and man shall not hurt nor destroy in all God's holy mountain. May we not hasten the day by bringing God's building on to His foundation, that its light may be like a city set on a hill.

Once more from our Patmos we glance back at the city of the great King, not to speak of its fall, but to examine its history while it yet entertained the witness and order of the new kingdom. They had been admonished that signs would take place, and fearful sights would be seen, and that high heaven would lend its warning to convince them of their folly.

The evidence of profane history is more credible with some men than the inspired record. Josephus their historian and the commander of their army in the defense of their city, testifies: "He states that a fiery sword in the character of a comet, hung over the city for a whole year."

That an extraordinary light appeared about the alter in the temple at the ninth hour of the night, making it as light as day. , That the massive gate of the interior eastern side of the temple, composed of solid brass, and of immense weight, requiring the strength of twenty men to make it fast, and secured with iron bolts, opened at the fifth hour of the night without human assistance, and was with great difficulty again closed.

That before the setting of the sun the appearance of chariots and armed men were seen in the air; in various places in the country, and passing around over the city.

The priests at the feast of Pentecost while employed in the duties of their office, were warned by a voice uttering distinctly the words, "let us begone; depart hence."

A prophet appeared in Jerusalem who continued for the space of more than three years to pronounce in a most earnest manner the words, "Woe to Jerusalem, to its temple, to the nation at large." And though punished often and with such severity that his bones were laid bare with the scourge; he neither wept, supplicated, nor protested; but between the strokes repeated his exclamation of woe to the city, until the siege was laid, and when upon the wall he was killed by a stone thrown from an engine.

The import of all these events, together with the overthrow of that nation point unerringly to the advent of a new authority, and a new order in the earth, the character and work of which will be more clearly seen in succeeding lectures.

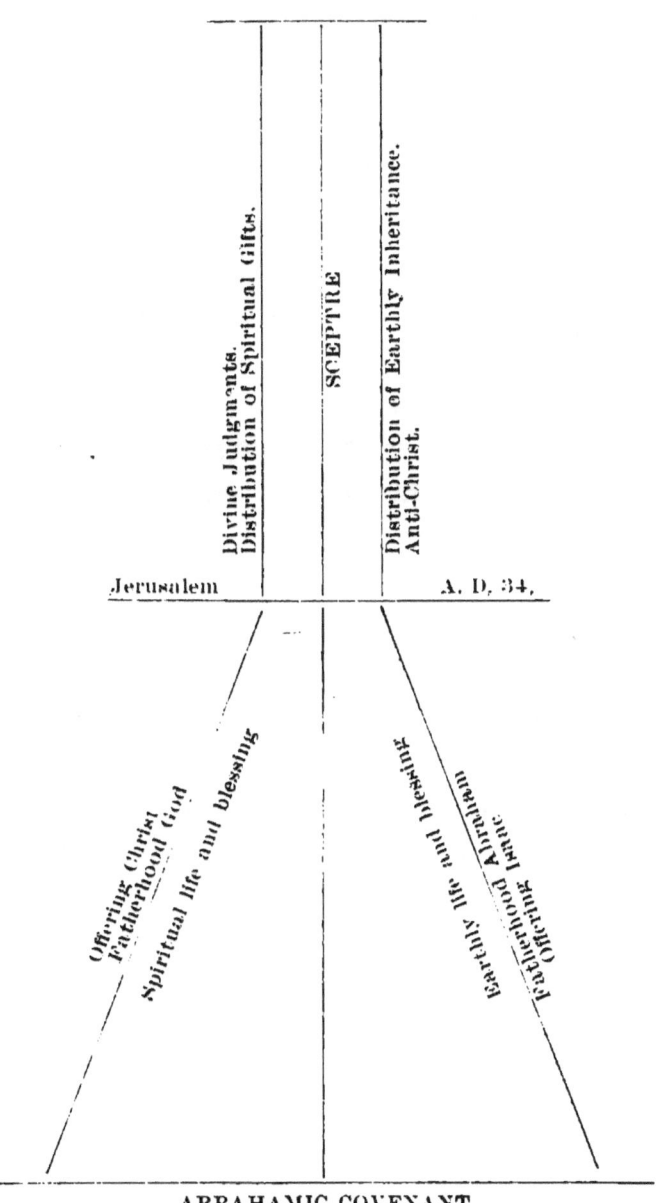

The Two Witnesses.

LECTURE SECOND,

THE MESSENGER OF THE COVENANT.

"Of the increase of his government and peace there shallbe no end, upon the throne of David and uponhis kingdom to order it, and establish it, with judgement and with justice, from henceforth even forever. The zeal of the Lord of Hosts will perform this." —Isa 9-7.

That "The Prince of the Kings of the earth" will perfectly execute any covenant ever ratified by God no one will doubt who believes He is the Son of God. He will in no way displace or annul the will of God or mar his authority.

Neither our Lord nor the Spirit that came in His name never exceeded the divine will in anything either taught, prophesied or done. It will be our effort to show clearly what constitutes the covenant under which his divine sceptre, is fashioned and wielded, and why the ordering of His kingdom is what we have found it to be. For this purpose let us look for His authority in its founding and order. He had said to the apostles, "I give unto you the keys" —not key but keys—"of the kingdom of heaven, and whatsoever thou shalt bind on earth shall be bound in heaven, and whatsoever thou shalt loose on earth shall be loosed in heaven."

What was to be done that would be binding between heaven and earth? The office of Christ as mediator in heaven and ruler in the earth and the terms of His mediation and the nature and character of His rule had to be established and proclaimed to all nations.

What had to be released? The authority God had given Moses the type of Christ had to be released, in order to give way for the sacrifice and law of Christ to become the arbitrer between God and all nations. Nothing but heaven's key, the Holy Ghost, could do this. Moses got his authority from a burning mountain, and its fundamental law was written on tables of stone he had hewn. But heaven had now established in the earth that authority which is cut out of the mountain without hands which must become "great and fill the whole earth." God is able to turn and overturn to make way for its triumph.

The dispensation by Moses regulated and established the relations of the people with God and with each other.

The dispensation by Christ regulates and establishes the relations of the people with God and with each other. Either is not a dispensation if they do not do both. It was dangerous to slight or trifle with the authority of Moses, and more dangerous to slight or trifle with the authority of Christ, for a greater than Moses is here.

The authority of high heaven never did, nor never will do any superfluous work. Divine authority is always exemplary, as in our Lord's baptism, institution of the supper, the washing of the disciples' feet; in fact His whole life is an example of what a restored humanity may become, but it cannot be attained simply by grace alone without the iron rule of His sceptre to eradicate from man's nature its own selfishness, and to remove from his spiritual life and its affinities the cause of its growth and power. That which makes the world what it is must have the same effect upon the church if it is not removed from its communion.

If we could get the scales from our eyes which world systems and world customs and world standards have glazed over them we would see that a dispensation that does not establish man's relation with man and adjust their rights so as to create a perfect brotherhood, could never lay claim to divine perfection. How could men become joint heirs with Christ and not become joint heir with his fellow man in the things which God has created? Does God's creation belong to God? If so could He make a company of worthy people his equal joint heirs and then recognize custom or law that would give to one of them the right and privilege of owning a whole continent or even a single state? That is just the principle Satan used in getting control of the kingdoms of this world, and joint heirship is just the principle Christ adopted to destroy all title He had to any part of it. Are we not forced to rely upon the power of the spirit and the truth for the renewing of our minds and purifying of our lives and hearts? If so are we to believe that the Spirit has left God's people a prey to that which has driven more people away from God than the truth has won to Him?

"And The Lord whom ye seek shall suddently come to His temple even the Messenger of the Covenant whom ye delight in. Behold He shall come saith The Lord but who shall abide the day of His coming? Who shall stand when He appeareth? For He is like a refiners fire and a Fuller's soap. And I will come near to you in judgement, I will be a swift witness against the sorcerers, adulterers, false swearers and against them that oppress the hireling in his wages, the widow and the fatherless and them that turn aside the stranger from his right and fear not me saith the Lord. Mal. 3—1-5."

Our Lord was the fulfillment of many promises and also of many prophecies. As the messenger of God's Covenant He came to lay in the earth, the great purpose of God's eternal plan, as the one sacrifice He entered into death once for all and "forever sat down on the right hand of the Majesty on high from thence forth expecting until His enemies be made His foot stool." For He must reign till He hath put all enemies under His feet. So His septre must now be lifted over the nations of the earth, demanding and inviting loyalty and cooperation in enlightening and redeeming man.

If the law of Christ did not inaugurate an operative plan of righteoussness specifically for His people, that would be a witness against sin and injustice. How does he expect His people to be practically righteous or exhibit the divine measure or standard? There is such a thing as begging our hope from Christ, and taking our standard from the world. There has been to much inviting and exhorting and condoling, and not enough building; too much professing and not enough living and being. We had better risk one living example of the spirit of God in defending and establishing righteousness, like the one which established joint heirship and spiritual cooperation at Jerusalem, than all the human opinions in the world. We are living and building wide of our privilege and sadly at variance with the message or testimony of this Messenger of the Covenant. There seems to be no visible distinct line between the righteousness of the churchand and righteousness of the world; there can be none, while the civilization of both rests on the same foundation and is conformed to the same standard.

"Therefore thus saitd the Lord; behold I lay in Zion for a foundation a stone, a tried stone, a precious corner stone—a sure foundation. He that believeth shall not make haste. Judgment also will I lay to the line, and righteousness to the plummet. The hail shall sweep away the reffuge of lies and water shall overfiow the hiding place."—Isa. 27: 16-17.

If we find the prophets in the foundation at Jerusalem we must receive their testimony as to the effect it would have. The righteousness established by the sceptre of Christ in this kingdom is seen to be perfectly upright as a plummet. It accorded the same right to all His subjects. The same law of induction into His kingdom—the same relation to God and to each other.

The world had never before received a dispensation which was upon all nations—addressed to all nations—and to which all nations are made accountable in the very constitution of it. To those who are looking for another, we enquire to what nation will it come, and what purpose will it serve?

This regulation in some things and indifference in other things leaves room for Satan to creep in and spoil everything.

God gave the world one inspired record of the divine constitution and building together of His kingdom, witnessed in his own way by his visible presence, written by its founders and builders, and He will not build over again; but will ere long enforce the sceptre of its authority over all men.

The world has trampled the foundation and building of His Son under its irreverent and reckless feet. Eighteen hundred years and the lease of its proud defiance will soon expire. Judgment has laid and will lay to the line ever since righteousness was established in the earth by the plummet of Christ's sceptre. Judgment stood like the horozontal end of a square to the planting of His sceptre in the overthrow of the typical nation and it lies today across the path of its antitype when the lease of their rule expires. The King has given to the world the witness of His own prophecy that when the record of its founding had reached all the nations the end of their lease would come, and that it would be trodden under foot to the end of that time.

His Right to its Sway.

The plea that will be entered against this two fold principle or law of joint heirship and its consequent enforcement will be that it appropriates to the benefit and use of others that which does not belong to them and to which they have no just right.

Let us see. It may be from your standpoint, not from His, nor from the nature of His work. He says to no one; I demand your wealth or you, or your service. No, my friend, he offers you himself, his life, his infinite resource of power—as having the keys of death and the grave with its dark and gloomy solitude. Heaven alone knows the darkness of that hour when the sun refused to shine, when the world in its madness cried "crucify him;" when in the agony of that hour he cried, "Father, forgive them, they know not what they do." Whose enemy was he meeting then? The same enemy he met in that forty days fast, who said, "All the kingdoms of the world will I give thee if thou wilt fall down and worship me." And to his honor and glory be it said that if there had been but one poor dying mortal to save, and that one you, he would not have done it. No, no, a thousand nos ring through the heavens now.

He asks; no, invites you; my fellow mortal; to come with yourself, with your substance, be it much or little, and cooperate, unite, be one with him, in redeeming yourself, and your fellow man, and the earth from the deadly clutch of his foe and yours, that you may share with him the abundance of his kingdom, and wear the eternal honors of a restored earth and race.

Would you deprive him the privilege in his kingdom of feeding the hungry, or rather preventing hunger, for we read of a time when they shall hunger and thirst no more. Charity, beneficence and protection has been awarded the province of earthly rule, and a worldly civilization. But it would be infinitely more to his honor if our Lord, who by his death and reign redeems man and his abode from death and the curse, if man brought to him the aid, power and influence of a divine civilization without the agencies which under the instigation of Satan, always have and always will poison it under imperfect rule and customs established by unrestrained human ambition; for God has chosen things that men dispise to confound the mighty.

The plan, then, of the divine empire is that of constitutional enactment legislative government and infalible promulgation followed and enforced by divine judgment. If uninspired, falible men can enact an imperfect constitution followed by imperfect legislation which is imperfectly understood, create accountibility, levy tribute, acquire domain, enforce its own form of rule and mould its own civilization and defend its own honor and authority, should we expect less of the corronated Christ?

If our own beloved nation, which has the best government ever inaugurated by man, has a right because of its inherent virtues, to displace Spain, and establish itself in Cuba, and if it is right in employing its own resources and people to an extent sufficient to accomplish that end, do we, can we, expect Christ to conquer Satan, banish evil, redeem and exalt man, abolish death and reinstate the Tree of Life, without an uncripled sceptre and the full extent of his authority in the institutions it uses and the agencies it employs. The longer the world lives the more it needs something above and beyond itself to save itself from its rapid rush in pursuit of its own ambition to save it from its own need, its own failures, its own mistakes and disappointments and the weight of its own woes?

The Covenant in the Sceptre.

The only covenant God ever confirmed with an oath in which he swore by himself, was the covenant conveying to the seed of Abraham the earth for an everlasting possession. For when righteousness by faith or through faith opened its door to all nations, through the promised seed which was Christ, it was put into his hands for execution that in him all the families of the earth might be blessed; and as Paul testifies, Abraham became heir of the world; it carries the covenant promise to all. When the reasons for this provision in God's eternal plan are seen, all questions and mysteries at once vanish. When we remember that through the resurrection earth's domain and its productions are inherited not by the living alone, but by all who share the blessed privilege of a resurrection through our Lord Jesus Christ. If joint heirship in things spiritual and things material be not an eternal principle in God's plan and the spiritual given supremacy over the natural, how can the earth be renewed by the New Heavens and made fit for the eternal tabernacle of God?

A mighty throng of the pure, the great, the good and the holy; who have suffered, wrought and toiled, and many who have given their lives, on the altar of the world's weal; among them your ancesters and kindred and mine; does the eternal plan of God give them only room and time in this world to toil, suffer and die? Thank God, His eternal plan never made them pilgrims and strangers in the earth while they were striving to be a world to God. It was because the world thought so much of itsself that even its Christ could find no place of birth in it but an inn. The resurrection will never bring a mighty host who are to be only invited guests while the nations bring their honor and glory into the "New Heavens" and the "New Earth." God is adding greatly to our glory and convenience just now by increased power, light and invention, and time only waits for all to be turned over to him of whose sceptre it is declared: "The kingdoms of this world have become the kingdoms of our Lord and of His Christ, and He shall reign forever and forever." (Ages on ages.)

As the nature of opposing powers are revealed in their war cry and methods of conquest, so the enlightenment of the day has placed the ban upon persecution and the spirit of cruel revenge as a means of extending power or securing sway.

The two witnesses and profance history alike wear the blush at the record of what corrupted human ambition will do to force its sway over man, his faith, his allegiance and inheritance. In weighing before the world's intelligence the sceptre of Christ and the very purest exhibition of human rule their contrast must be exhibited; their purpose and province be seen in order that their right of sway in the earth may be awarded.

It is just and fair for the writer to correct false conceptions and erroneous ideas of the divine rule in the earth. As to the character of its opposition the world needs no revelation. It has much to its credit; but very little but what is the result of the divine leaven that truth has given it. The world has borrowed its hope from Christ and guilded its justice with a pretense that it conformed to the righteousness of His rule.

From a careful study of the whole plan as revealed in the two witnesses, we fail to account for the failure of the mass of its readers and students to grasp its purpose, and the end and aim of its remedial agencies.

That its grand beneficient purpose, with all the means employed, relate to the recovery of man from sin and its penalty, death; and the removal of the curse and man's exaltation to his promised dominion over the works of a divine creation in the restored relation of communion with God.

Paul in the second of Hebrews connects the sceptre of Christ directly with this purpose as above defined. We quote God's approval of His Son when he says: "A sceptre of righteousness is the sceptre of thy kingdom," and adds, "For unto the angels hath he not put in subjection the world to come, whereof we speak." But one in certain place testifies: "What is man that thou art mindful of him, or the son of man that thou visiteth Him?" "Thou hast put all things under his feet; thou hast left nothing that is not put under Him." In these quotations we find a clear foundation for the promise of Christ, oft repeated, that saints should be kings and priests unto God.

No one will deny man's fitness for such a relation to God and His works when he has attained to a state of perfect righteousness. And we premise here that he will have attained that state when his nature is so renewed that he loves God with all the affections of his nature, and his fellow man to the same extent he loves himself. For on these two characteristics of fundamental divine law hang all the law and the prophets.

In order to plant in man's nature the ground for perfecting this love to God, He exhibits to man his love in the gift of His Son for man's redemption brings man into sonship and heirship with their Redeemer and imparts to man the spirit of His Son.

In order to plant in man's nature the ground for the perfecting of this love for his fellow man He institutes the relation of equal joint heirship to man's inheritance, thus removing all obstacles to a perfect brotherhood in the great and glorious family of God. Hence the twofold relation man sustains would be brought into perfect harmony with God's perfect law and the tabernacle (meeting place) of God could be restored in the earth and rest with man.

It is important that we find the real cause of the bitterness in the vision of this conflict outlined in the repeated prophecy and in which the two witnesses take on sackcloth and increased power.

It was not because of any weakness or imperfection in the divine sceptre for it is in the hands of the Prince of the Kings of the earth, and the Soverign of the universe is bound by solemn covenant to enforce it.

When the sceptre has been planted in the earth in the typical city with that nation which has been previously prepared by sufficient light and proclamation of its authority for its reception, and it was rejected, judgment speedily followed and the nation was overthrown.

At this point in repeated prophecy it stands in challenge before all nations for their acceptance and adoption. To them the same stone has become the head of the corner. But the nations must first be fully admonished by divine proclamation of its founding, character and object; and when the two witnesses have finished their work of witnessing—as testified by its King—the work of judgment must and will follow. But the nations will treat the sceptre and the two witnesses as the typical nation treated its King—overcome and kill them.

We cannot emphasize too forcibly that the opposition is all on the part of man, and something in man's nature and customs that the sceptre challenges and interupts. In this age as in that it is not the person of Christ or His work, for that the world admires. It is now and always has been that in man's nature which alienates man. The spirit of monopoly with which unrestrained ambition clothes the province of human nature, and prompts man to a ceaseless struggle to gain ascendency over his brother man, and over a just equilibrium of right pertaining to anything. The chief hindrance in the way of the divine sceptre, then and now, is the world's ignorance of and opposition to, the complete brotherhood of man, the foundation for which we find laid in His kingdom at its founding at Jerusalem. Earthquake after earthquake (revolutions) have passed in review before the plain testimony of the two witnesses while the world has closed its ear to their faithful testimony; and has rushed madly on in its path of warfare, bloodshed and suffering.

The world must learn the primary lesson that in God's revelation concerning His Son it must find its path and its means to rest and glory; and not in the biased judgment or opinions of men.

If we could induce the misguided church of today to bring up to the present the unrecognized part of that foundation which provided for, and exhibited to the gaze of assembled nations the restored brotherhood of man and again build together the earthly and spiritual foundation of a holy temple in the Lord, it would be a work of more value than a thousand lives like our own.

The sceptre has been called a sceptre of mercy. It is more. It is a leader, a regenerator and a renewer. "Ye shall know the truth and the truth shall make you free." "Old things have passed away, all things have become new." The plan committed to the sceptre preceeds judgment and when its irom rule is disclosed, as it will be, it will smite the nations and exhibit the injustice, false pride, arrogance, and false claims to righteousness in their deceived and misguided position before the true standard.

When the world discovers that it has stumbled at that stumbling stone and rock of offense, which was laid at Jerusalem that made all men equal in right and appropriation, it found resistance in the will that could only find gratification in a struggle for supremacy.

When man aspires to a new birth and life, the power that gives him that birth and conducts him in the attainment of that life; must provide for his return to the childhood of his nature for self-renunciation, and for such safe conduct of life as will ward off the necessity for its return. The failure of the church to discover and apply the provision in the kingdom for these ends, has filled it with dissatisfied hopes and weak and vascillating lives, and Christlike life and strength is sacrificed.

The world and the church today sadly needs the exemplary and demonstrative power of such a divine civilization as the building of God on His perfect foundation could furnish. The world is wiser in its day than the Children of Light. Its carnal spirit has discovered the vast advantage in cooperation to attain its own ends; but where is the institution today that can point to the application of the command of the Spirit that there be no divisions among you, but to be perfectly joined together, in the same mind and the same judgment? Can we imagine that Christ prayed for the unity and cooperation of His body, and did not provide for its unity and cooperation?

The sceptre intercepts judgment. Its conditional grace and favor make it available. Judgment is alike progressive and corrective. What force these facts have upon us as a people as the conflict of ages draws nearer its final contest and decisive measure of strength.

If the authority of Christ, embracing as it does, all power in heaven and earth, has in it the foundation truths underlying a perfect state it must and will prevail. If a system, a rule, or a faith; be fundamentally wrong, it never can be made practically right. To use Christ's own figure; "If the tree be corrupt its fruit will be corrupt."

A system or rule that is based on a false or incorrect foundation will need constant amending and propping to make it bearable and practically applicable to its purpose. These constant additions and subtractions make it top heavy and so cumbersome that neither wealth nor wisdom can maintain it and it falls of its own weight. The things that are transitory cannot be eternal. "These things must be once more shaken that the things that cannot be shaken may remain."

If God could have saved man and accommodate His plan to any, or all, other ideas of what it might be, the world would have been saved long ago, and much of suffering averted. But His plan is perfect and will in the most available auspicious time accomplish its beneficient purpose.

The prophecy in Danial in regard to the four universal empires and particularly the fourth, or Gentile rule. the character and nature of which is set forth in Daniel 7:7; is brought forward in the vision of John and repeated again before "many nations, kindreds and tongues." The repeating of this prophecy gives to inspired prophecy the testimony of history as it records their rise, reign and overthrow by their successors, and thus confirms before the world the testimony of the two witnesses.

The prophecy of the revelator exhibits in forcast the history of the fourth empire and the limit of its triumph over the witnesses, and its apparent victory over the secptre of the man Child who was to rule all nations with a rod of iron. The standpoint of this prophecy enables the revelator to outline and describe the then future fortunes of the church and the character and strength of its opposition.

The destructive malignant character and work of this fourth universal empire has passed into history, and the limit also of its power over the two witnesses carries us back to the work of Luther Tyndale and other translators. The eminent work of our modern bible societies has given world wide distribution of the bible in the different languages of the world. With the bible in one hand and profane history in the other we can look back at the reign of death. and darkness, and through the revelator look forward to the glorious triumph of the kingdom of our Lord. Time only waits for the announcement, "That the kingdoms of this world have become the kingdoms of our Lord and of His Christ, and that He shall reign forever and forever."

We may very easily and unpurposely impeach the testimony of the two witnesses, in the attitude we assume toward the work assigned them and the manner in which that work has been done. It has been their province to witness the creation of the earth and of man with the avowed purpose of letting him have dominion over it; and to witness the transgression of man by assuming the right to appropriate to his use its fruits that he did not need and could not appropriate to his benefit.

For this reason and no other, the spontaneous productiveness of the earth in the things that were best for the sustainance of man was interupted and noxious needless productions substituted. This is declared to be the nature of the curse promounced upon it. The serpent, which is the personification of evil and of God's enemy and also man's, tempts man with the spirit of coveteousness—discontent with what God provided for him—and thus we find the very foundation laid in man's nature for that which has been his greatest foe. It has made him a slave and menial, and as the ages wear away becomes more and more exacting.

Because of Satan's intrusion upon man's property and safe relations to God's creation, God predicted that the seed of the woman should bruise the serpent's head. No one can reasonably suppose that man, corrupted by habitual indulgence in self gratification of this same propensity, would ever formulate and adopt a principle that could eradicate from man's nature one so dominating as the world has seen this one to be? But the wisdom of God could see the remedy and predict its application even to the arch deceiver who aroused in man that power he possessed to exercise a coveteous desire for that he did not need.

It becomes necessary to go back to the advent of evil and its fearful consequences, to ascertain the danger point in man's nature as well as to discover the advent of the remedial system found in the two witnesses. We note that man would possess very little to distinguish him as the highest work of the creation if he did not possess the power of violation and aggressiveness in the pursuit of his personal ambition.

But when those powers become the seat of a principle foreign to a perfect constitution of his nature and makes his ambition the agent of self to that extent that he cannot preserve intact the natural relation of a common brotherhood, they place him at varience with the fundamental law of universal right.

So we find in the record of the two witnesses that God chose a righteous representative of our race, made covenant with him, that he should be the father of many nations, and to a nation of his descendants he gave a law written on tables of stone. The nation was typical in the sense that through them he would preserve his own record of his authority and the measures taken to fulfill his promises. The law was written by God himself on Mount Sivrai; the mountain typified the high authority, and the tables signifying its divine nature or infallible rule of conduct. It defined the duty of man toward God, and also the duty of man toward his fellow man. Its substance covers what man should worship, and what he should allow his nature to indulge or prompt him to desire or do. We see that the aim of divine government is the exaltation of man in his affectional and practical nature. If man could have attained true moral greatness and excellence as well by indulgence as by positive restraint, God would have left him free to exercise his own discretion; but a state of human perfection and communion with God would never be attained.

The divine authority is prohibitory; but divine grace is reclaiming and saving in its aims and since "the law was given by Moses, but grace and truth came by Jesus Christ." Christ goes beyond the "Thou shalt not" and places man in such a relation to God and his fellow man that He has no temptation to false worship or to covet anything of an earthly nature. He positively declared that to those who "sought first the kingdom and its righteousness all these things should be added," which He could not have promised if the kingdom did not contain them.

In the light of God's plan as revealed in both the old and new dispensations He reserves to himself the right to rule and care for his own people. He is able, willing and entirely prepared to do so when men get in that position that they can appropriate His matchless favor.

Christ is a great economist and furnishes His saints not what the world calls a free government at a burdensome cost of millions annually; but a perfect government free. He does not employ a world full of machinery to administer government to a righteous people. His plan brings men into the righteousness of His kingdom, where they become kings and priests unto God in the things of this world. They constitute the nobility of the kingdom of heaven. And why should they not; for the constitution of His kingdom gives them the opportunity to build states without prison walls, hospitals, asylumns, court houses and legislatures. These implements and devices are indispenseable where corrupting agencies and institutions feed the passions of degenerate man; but the body of the risen Christ is not left by its head either to be exposed to the insideous influences of exemplary vice, or a part of a system or custom that approves or upholds it. He could not have them "grow up into Him in such relations."

Just prior to the time John wrote this revelation the two witnesses had become incarnated in human flesh. The Old Testament in the person of John, the forerunner, and the New Testament in the person of Christ, the mediator. These two remarkable persons proclaimed the immediate advent of the kingdom of heaven; and divine manifestations bear abundant testimony to the reality of their predictions.

This power or process of incarnation in the human mind the truth in its purity, and man's capacity to receive, is the evidence that the recovery of the race is possible and the reason that the "Word was made fiesh and dwelt amoung us," and we beheld its "Glory reflected in man."

The possibility of man's reasoning powers becoming invested with truth without mixture of error, and the resurrection power of the Creator stands in God's foundation like a mighty rock against which infidelity and all the combined forces of deceptive power will be hurled in vain. There is hope for a man's recovery as long as his mind is open to receive truth and his conscience responds to its appeal.

If man's relations in the world are of that character that he drinks in more of the world's deceptions and unnecessary philosophy than God's eternal and revealed truth, his recovery from the dominion of evil can never under these conditions become complete.

For this reason as well as many others, the kingdom of Christ in its founding emancipated man from the fearful neccessity of living amid a mountain of uncertainty and seeking to flash through its cloud of mists the light of divine life while his own mind and life must partake of its deception. It would be entirely useless for the perfect Christ to invest his people with a perfect standard and not provide for gathering them together under that standard. When the possibility and feasibility of the complete incarnation of the pure living truth stands exemplified in the person of every man who first received and wrote it for the enlightenment of the world, who will dare attempt to measure our responsibility, with the fact standing out boldly before us that our attitude toward the kingdom of Christ is still leaving these two witnesses of the living Christ with the shade of mourning that our indifference casts upon them?

If we follow the prophetic vision of John in its outline of events yet future, we behold the two witnesses in the majesty of their power and might. Their garb of mourning has been cast aside and robed in white, they advance rapidly on to the work of conquest.

They have long been treated by a world seeking age, as a kind of secondhand necessity, as embodying a hope for man but dimly seen. The increasing light of the present time is revealing to many the exceeding strength and obdurancy of organized evil and injustice and the vast chasm unbridled ambition and a fluctuating standard of justice has left between the wealthy and the poor; and multiplied expedients are proposed to remedy our ills and ward off our dangers and our liabilities.

The fact that there is but one remedy, that forever settles perfectly and forever man's relation with a Creator and His creation; and that relation defined by unerring justice must find recognition and acceptance, seems not to have occured to the world in its thought upon these mighty problems.

Two things pertaining to this witness ought to attract universal attention and enquiry. The first is that the nations have been deceived, and the prophecy unveils to man the nature of the deception. In the ending of the conquest by the "Two Witnesses" they

THE TWO WITNESSES. 55

invite the fowls of heaven to a great supper of God Almighty that they may eat the flesh (carnal appetites) of kings and captains and mighty men and the flesh of horses and their riders. (The work of conquest by opposing powers).

When we see these are overtaken and also the false prophet which had deceived them, and their deceptions together with their titles and high rank is cast into a lake of fire for their consumption, we must reason that these purely carnal achievements and the distinctions they create did not exist by the authority of the conquering power which is called the "Word of God." If the rod of iron which is to rule in their stead and which preceeds from the Word and smites the nations had not been disclosed to the nations and presented to them by the Word they could not have been deceived.

On the other hand, if the iron rule had been established in the earth and had been proclaimed by the conquering power, then the fleshy character of worldly rule and the distinctions and titles of worldly customs did not exist only by assumed right.

The Open Book.

LECTURE THIRD.

"And I wept much because no man was found worthy to open and to read the book; neither to look thereon." Rev. 5:4.

Again we take our standpoint of observation eighteen centuries ago, aside the apostle John in his Patmos; and see a door opened in heaven. And one sat on the throne. This, the throne of the universe had never been abdicated by the Creator of all things; and there never will cease to be voices and thunderings as long as disorder and imperfection casts its shadow upon the sceptre of the universe. The four beasts full of eyes behind and before cast their crowns before God's throne and declared that He is worthy to receive honor and glory, for He had created all things for his pleasure. No well ordered intelligence can rest in disorder for order is Heaven's first law.

The author of these lectures cannot be loyal to the "Prince of the Kings of the earth" without refuting one gross and widespread error, and one which he fears will bring wrath upon nations, ecclesiastical bodies and individuals. That is, that in the constitution of his kingdom as recorded in the Acts of His Apostles, He does not so clearly define and exhibit his authority as to supercede the right of any other rule in the earth from the time of His exaltation to authority, until all foes become His footstool. If He did not establish in the constitution of His kingdom such authority, He is unworthy to be king; for he boldly declared to his apostles that all power was given unto him in heaven and earth; and sent them to proclaim His kingdom to all nations and to every creature.

"And a throne was set in heaven." A throne signifies highest in authority. As to setting of this new throne at the right hand of God, it was set when the heir to the throne of David ascended to the right hand of God. This we prove by Peter, when the Holy Ghost with fiery tongue proclaimed to all nations His exaltation at the right hand of God; A. D. 33; recorded in Acts 2:34.36.

"For David is not ascended into the heavens but David saith himself; the Lord said unto my Lord, "Sit thou on my throne, until I make thy foes thy footstool."

Peter then testified he is at the right hand of God, exalted and made both Lord and Christ. From that time this fact became the foundation store in the constitution of his kingdom, and whatever he commands must be obeyed So we find in the right hand of God a book; that bood opened would reveal his infinite displeasure with all that mared or defiled his perfect work. The book was written within and on the back side, sealed with seven seals. No man is found able to break the seals or worthy to open and read the book.

The book here held in the right hand of God will not be needed when God is all in all, which will be the case when the "Prince of the Kings of the earth" delivers his sceptre back to His Father; having first subdued all things opposed to the will, or authority, or pleasure of God. In as much as Jesus Christ, who is a mediator between man the creature and God the Creator, undertakes to restore man to his allegiance to God, and bring the blessings of the infinate Creator upon all his works; he is worthy to receive God's revelation of his own character, attributes and disposition toward man.

The seals and writing within and on the back side make it imperative that the book be opened and read. Back at the creation when the old serpent succeeded in introducing evil and a consequent penalty of death and curse upon the earth, God made a prediction, viz:

"That man should bruse the serpent's head, while the serpent would bruise man's heel." The serpent's posterity and man's posterity were to be at emnity. When or how the serpent's head was to be bruised, did not appear in the prediction. But the prediction is written in the book. No one from the back of the book could possibly uuderstand what the prediction implied in detail. When God called Abraham to leave the land of Ur, and promised to make of him a multitude of nations, and that in his posterity all the familes of the earth should be blessed. From that standpoint it was impossible to see when and how the promise would be fulfilled.

When God made choice of twelve of Abraham's descendants to be the heads of the twelve tribes of a great nation, no one could see just what it had to do with the covenant made with Abraham—making him heir of the world. It was then impossible to see in what way that would carry out the promise.

When the posterity of the twelve Patriarchs were in bondage four hundred and thirty years in Egypt, and were brought out under the leadership of Moses, God's promises were still shrouded in mystery. When the nation had been established in their Canan, and the prophets still repeated the promises of a coming heir to the throne of David, and prophesied of the sufferings of Christ, and the glory that should follow, we find them searching diligently what manner of time the spirit of Christ which was in them did signify; and angels desiring to look into the fulfillment of their wonderful predictions.

Whenever promises or prophecies are fulfilled, and the events or circumstances occuring are pointed out as their fulfillment by the one who was found worthy to loose the seals and open the book; then those promises—prophecies—together with the plan they accomplish, as recorded in the history of the events themselves, are no longer sealed. Fulfillment unseals the prophecies and events unfold the plan.

In the birth and life of John, the forerunner and proclaimer of the immediate coming of the kingdom of heaven, and the birth, life and work and subsequent death, resurrection, ascention and coronation of the Christ, has taken place. These events open the book and unfold the mysteries which had been hid from ages, but was then made known to his holy apostles. So the Lamb on Mount Zion prevailed to open the book and loose the seals thereof.

Other characters are given prominence in the visions of John and deserve recognition here. Their interest at the throne and in the Lamb, seem to have elevated them to a seat near the throne. They had crowns of gold; a symbol of high honor in the exercise of authority, proceeding from the throne itself. Lexicons upon the Title Elder say their authority was almost unlimited under, or next to constitutional law; that they acted as judges, sitting in the gates of the local cities.

The office of Elder in the kingdom of Christ as overseers of its interests brings rulers to the level of its subjects so far as worldly honors are concerned. The only honors accorded were spiritual, and they were to be merited by humble service to the subjects of the king. Heaven never questions the wisdom of making the office of Elder the highest ruling authority among the earthly subjects of his kingdom, but provides seats for them near the throne. Many earthly rulers of great distinction soon would be glad to exchange offices for this one if it would give them the same recognition in heaven that Elders receive.

The adoption of this rule in his kingdom justifies the king; for when He was here as heir to the throne of the universe, He gave the founders of His kingdom a most astounding lesson of what would bring them enduring honor in heaven and earth. He took water and washed their feet. Peter objected, but submitted and took the lesson. If I your Lord and Master. Oh how humble, yet how perfect is the sceptre of the king of all the earth. How perfect is the divine constitution under which His sceptre is weilded.

The objection may be made that overseers as a ruling authority does not appear in the record of the founding of the kingdom at Pentecost, as recorded in Acts; second and third chapters. But listen to the apostle Peter, through whom the gospel of the kingdom was then revealed: "The Elders which are among you I exhort. Who am also an Elder, and a witness of the suffering of Christ. Feed the flocks of God, taking the oversight thereof." Not as Lords over God's heritage, but being examples of flocks;" or again, "Obey them that have the rule over you, and submit for they watch for your souls."

But remember it was the Holy Ghost which Christ said the father would send, in His name, which gave to the subjects of the kingdom its overseers, and the kind and order of its ordinances, and the conduct of its temporal and spiritual interests.

Humanity precedes exaltation in the kingdom of heaven. It is important just here that we introduce (the four beasts full of "eyes before and behind" and have eyes within) to the notice of the reader. For John sees these beasts cast their crowns before the throne in heaven. These beasts undoubtedly represent the four universal empires which prophecy declares will be succeeded and completely displaced by the Lion of the tribe of Judah, who succeeds to universal empire—all these empires, viz: The Babylonian, Medo Persian, Grecian and Roman, are all prophetically warned of their becoming like the chaff of the summer threshing floor, driven away by the wind, and a stone cut out of the mountain (throne of the universe) without hands, should become a great mountain (authority) and fill the whole earth. So John is permitted to see them worship before the throne in heaven.

The beasts are in the midst of a sea of glass, (a multitude of people) which represents the position of the four empires to the worship of the true God; the last of the four having the sceptre at the time the kingdom of Christ was established at Jerusalem. At the opening of the seals they invite attention to the work of their empire, and horses symbolizing the character and purpose of their reign, and the result of their conquests.

For the purpose of this lecture it is only neccessary to deal briefly with the fourth empire in its relation to the kingdom of Christ. The opening of the fourth seal discloses a pale horse, and his name that sat on him was Death. Power was given to him to make war upon the saints, and to overcome them. No doubt the world will be permitted to see the worst and the best of human rule. Its history contains a falling away, a bloody reign and a kind of reformation.

We may readily infer from all we have seen of the character of the "Prince of the Kings of the earth" and the constitution of His kingdom, that His authority in regulating the earthly affairs of His subjects, had to be cast aside, and human policy, human ambition, pride, arrogance and assumption of individual right substituted, in order to prosecute the kind of rule ascribed to the fourth and last empire. A king who places all the interests of his subjects, both religious and secular, in the hands of those whose only motive in ruling is love and who never can become more than a joint heir with their fellow subjects to rewards, emoluments, need have no fear that his sceptre will be dripping with the blood and suffering of his subjects. No danger of hunger, famine, poverty and starvation where all have the same right to the blessings of high heaven.

We venture the suggestion that man has suffered more from man of all that is here described as the work of Gentile dominion, than under any other empire in the world. If we had the sum of its martyrs, of innocents tortured, of its millions starved with hunger, of its millions sacrificed to defeat the ungodly ambitions of some other self imposed monarch; the degredation, the unrequited toil, the grinding poverty and the corroding care, from Nebuched Nezzar's time down to the present time; all of which can be seen to be the fruit of the right to individual supremacy, we would not wonder that the opening of the fifth seal exhibited their souls (lives) as crying with a loud voice: "How long; How long?" Oh Lord, dost thou not avenge our blood on them that dwell on the earth; nor that white robes were given them, and they were invited to reign with their suffering but coronated Lord.

With deepest awe, and yet with love for our fellow man, we approach the opening of the sixth seal.

"And lo, there was a great earthquake, (revolution) and the sun became black as sackcloth and the moon as blood, (no light in the political or ecclesastical heaven) and the kings of the earth and the great men, and the chief captains, and the mighty men, bond men and free men hide themselves, calling for rocks and mountains to fall on them and hide them from the wrath of the Lamb; for the great day of his wrath had come, and who shall be able to stand?"

Oh how many will fail to receive the seal of the living God in their foreheads? Why not bow to the sceptre of your King; reinstate the perfect order of His kingdom? The king is holding out His sceptre; the earth praying for it; a groaning creation is demanding it; human suffering pleads for it; bewildered minds grope to understand it, and pride and mere human ambition denies it. Heaven weeps over man,s unwillingness. The coming of this day of wrath upon the nations is justified by their indiference to, and their rejection of the sceptre of the "Prince of the Kings of the earth."

The wrath upon the typical nation of the Jews, was of itself sufficient as a national warning of their fate if they rejected the "stone which had become the head of the corner" and which ground the typical nation to powder. And farther, because all men ought to expect and be willing that the sceptre of Christ should enforce and carry into effect the two cardinal principles of the unchangable law of God. viz: "Thou shalt love the Lord thy God with all thy might, mind and strength, and thy neighbor as thyself."

Upon these two hang all the law and the prophets; and in the constitution of His kingdom at Jerusalem, Christ put into effect that which perfectly carries out the unchangable law of God. He did this by making all equal in right and title under his sceptre. The justice and purity of these two cardinal principles are acknowledged by all enlightened men. It is their practical application to all men by the "Prince of the Kings of the earth," by placing all His subjects on one common level in regard to possessions or honors, that offends nations and individuals.

But it might be affirmed just here that if human selffshness, greed and human ambition enthroned, begets crime, tolerates murder, robbery, drunkenness, prostitution, theft and extortion, it ought to be shut out of every constition of every government in heaven and earth. Here is just why the sceptre of Jesus Christ will cast down the wrath of God upon the world for the righteous blood it has shed. And which will be severest upon teachers and builders for rejecting the divine foundation which rests upon apostles and prophets. Christ being the chief corner stone. It is the inforcement of this sceptre which will convulse the nations and produce the great earthquake (revolution) which will dissolve and displace the corrupt rule of the earth. The masses, when they see, as all will see, that the rule to which they have been subjected does not exist by divine right, but has existed by divine forbearance only, will rally to the sceptre of the "Prince of the Kings of the earth."

After they have been sealed in their foreheads, as appears under the opening of the sixth seal. "They appear a great multitude which no man can number of all nations, people, kindreds and tongues, stood before the Lamb with palms in their hands, (emblem of victory) and clothed in the robe of righteousness." These, as seen, come out of the great tribulation because of their having been sealed. "They hunger no more, neither thirst any more, for the Lamb in the midst of the throne is leading them."

At the opening of the seventh and last seal there is silence in heaven for a brief space of time. But seven angels are given seven trumpets, but before they are permitted to sound much incense is added to the prayers of saints, and the smoke of the incense ascended up before God. The censer is filled with fire off the altar and cast into the earth, and there were voices and thunderings and an earthquake.

In order to prove that the author has made no mistake in the interpretation of the earthquake which the opening of the seventh seal discloses, and which results from fire off the altar being cast into the earth; that it means such a revolution, peaceful or otherwise, as will break into pieces world powers and all opposition to the kingdom of the "Prince of the Kings of the earth," he calls in the testimony of the now open book which sends out its seven trumpets to announce the way in which the great day of His wrath will convulse the earth.

When God gave the typical nation of the Jews their law, He sanctified that authority by a trumpet which sounded long and loud; the mount was burning with fire, there was darkness, blackness and a tempest, and the voice then speaking shook the earth. The apostle declares that the subjects of Christ's kingdom are not called to witness the thunders of Sinai, but that they have come to to the city of the living God, the New Jerusalem. Heb. 12:18-29. And adds: "See that you refuse not Him that speaketh, for if they escaped not who refused him that speaketh on earth, much more shall not we escape if we turn away from Him that speaketh from heaven, whose voice then shook the earth." But now He hath promised, saying once more; "I shake not the earth only, but heaven." The apostle says this once more signifies the removing of the things that are shaken as of things that are made, that the things which cannot be shaken may remain

Wherefore we, receiving a kingdom which cannot be moved; let us have grace whereby we may serve God acceptably. Here the apostle declares that the present heaven (political and ecclesastical powers) and the earth, (present organized order) will be removed and that the kingdom of Christ cannot be moved. One more apostolic witness found in Second Peter, 3:10-13. He says the day of the Lord will come as a thief in the night, in which the heavens will pass away with a great noise, (comotion) and the elements shall melt with fervent heat; and that the removing of the present heaven and earth will be followed with the new heaven and the new earth wherein dwelleth righteousness.

The author cannot pass from these witnesses without justifying his construction upon the fire cast off the altar into the earth. By the open book it will be seen that fire and firey events and burning consumption are terms in which prophetic announcement of divine judgments are made. The prophet Joel says of the day of wrath, "It will burn as an oven, and all the proud and the wicked will be as stubble." Paul says, "every man's work on the divine foundation shall be tried as by fire." And again "Our Lord is a consuming fire." John the Baptist says, "every tree that bringeth not forth good fruit shall be cast into the fire." Jude in his book of a single chapter, being the last of the Epistelary writings, describes this day of wrath by a quotation from the prophets, and we here give his language: "Behold the Lord cometh with ten thousand of His saints to execute judgment upon all, and to convince all that are among them of all their ungodly deeds which they have committed; and of all their hard speeches which ungodly sinners have spoken against Him. These are murmerers complainers walking after their own lusts, and their mouth speaketh great swelling words, having men's persons in admiration, because of advantage.

The effect of divine wrath is most clearly defined at the giving of the law to God's typical people, and recorded in the 28th chapter of Deuteronomy.

The reader is requested to read Deuteronomy 28th chapter, as the character and effect of divine judgment is there fully described. All of which we see carried out in the history of that typical nation and their remarkable overthrow. It will be remembered that Christ in His propecies respecting the final judgment upon that nation, mingled with it His prophecies respecting the judgments upon all nations at the end of Gentile dominion, and stated that the gospel of the kingdom must first be published among all nations; then the end would come.

He also stated that there would be signs in sun, moon and stars, and upon the earth distress of nations, with perplexity, the sea and waves roaring; men's hearts failing them for fear, and for looking for those things to come on the earth, for the powers of heaven shall be shaken.

Unless the divine judgment upon that nation which received first the sceptre of the "Prince of the Kings of the earth" was highly exemplary and typical of divine judgment upon all nations for rejecting that sceptre, the author can see no reason for His connecting the two great events effecting His kingdom.

We have the strongest evidence of this fact in the records of God's commands in regard to the character required in any king that He would ever choose or permit to reign over Israel. We quote Deuteronomy 17;15-20. "The Lord thy God shall choose one from thy brethren; And that his heart be not lifted up above his brethren; and that he turn not aside from the commandment to the right or to the left. Stephen, the first martyr under the sceptre of Christ, identifies Christ as the anti-type of Moses, and states that whosoever will not obey Him shall be cut off from among His people.

In support of the position that the seven trumpets describe the divine judgment which will characterize the great day of wrath. The author calls attention to the fact that the opening of the seven seals, the sounding of the seven trumpets and the pouring out of the seven vials of wrath, all terminate at one terminal point.

The seventh seal discloses an earthquake, a "shaking of the powers of the heavens," caused by fire from off the altar. Rev. 8:4-5. The sounding of the seventh trumpet announces two terminal events. The first of these two is proclaimed by the angel having in his hand the open book, and setting one foot on the sea and the other on the earth, proclaimed with a loud voice, swearing by Him that liveth forever that time as declared by the prophets and measured by the mystery of God, should be finished when the seventh trumpet begins to sound. Then as the measure of prophetic time relating to the kingdom of Christ expires, the sounding of the seventh trumpet proclaims that the "Kingdoms of the world are become the kingdoms of our Lord and His Christ, and He shall reign forever and forever." (Ages on ages.) The foes of Christ have become His footstool.

In His message to the churches, in the open book, nor in the sounding of the seventh trumpet, is there any intimation that His sceptre has changed or been modified since He sat down at the right hand of God, A. D. 33. The same order, ordinances, gifts and blessings pertain to it still.

His kingdom presented an open door to the seven churches of Asia. That door was opened when He sat down at the right hand of God, A. D. 33; is open now, and will remain open until the nations walk in the light of it, and bring their honor and glory into it. Its gates are never shut day or night, only against that which works abomination or introduces falsehood.

The apostle in writing his Revelation was to write of the things that were and the things that should be thereafter. Of the things that were then the "Prince of the Kings of the earth" discloses the mystery of the iniquity already working, and in His sevenfold warning holds out to the churches (local assemblies of His subjects) the exaltation of their king and vividly portrays the power of His sceptre. The open book alike testifies that He held the sceptre against which nothing could prevail, and that it never failed to furnish its might to those who took refuge under it.

There is one painful case among the seven which the author cannot pass and discharge the high responsibility he has taken upon him. It is the last of the seven. We find there the conditions which always have and always will come squarely between the province and beneficense of the king and His subjects.

"I know thy works that thou art neither hot nor cold. "Because thou sayest I am rich and increased in goods, and have need of nothing; and knowest not that thou art wretched, and miserable, and blind, and poor, and naked. I counsel thee to buy of me gold tried in the fire, that thou mayest be rich; and white raiment, that thou mayest be clothed "Ye cannot serve

God and Mammon," has been His bold and emphatic declaration.

That no man could serve two masters He very well knew, for he would hold to the one and dispise the other. Such had been proven to be the case with the Laodiceans; such has always been the case with churches, with nations and individuals. And if the "Prince of the Kings of the earth" had not shut out of his kingdom the liability to stumble over the stumbling block of the very root of all evil, He could not have justly spued out the Laodiceans. He could not with consistency have made the straight path to exaltation in His kingdom, the result of His own beneficience, and power, and the medium of God's infinite blessing, and at the same time allow the subjects of His kingdom to bow to the behests of the mannon of unrighteousness, either to climb upward among their fellows or to procure their sustenance.

He that could feed five thousand with five loaves and two fishes, will always be able to feed his subjects without their being burdened with such individual care and effort as to render them almost oblivious to all that is really great and ennobling.

He well knew that if he left the door open for covetousness to become enthroned in human hearts, it would be the stepping stone to man worship, and even permit wealth to buy its way to rule; and human systems would even inaugurate the worst corruptions for gain.

The author would not for one moment cast any approbrium upon honest persevering effort, nor disregard the need or merit of persevering industry; but he has resting upon him responsibility that should make him oblivious to unjust criticism. If he may be able to point out to his fellow man clearly and unmistakably, the sceptre of him of whom Moses and the prophets did write; if his feeble effort may soften judgment, avert calamity, quiet unrest and strife, dethrone evil, and banish human suffering, he would have accomplished a task worth a thousand such lives as his own. If the conditions now do not demand the sceptre they never have. If the remedy it affords cannot be applied by this enlightened age, then the author dispairs of his fellows staying or softening the day of wrath.

The exercise of all the powers of man in attaining either wealth or mere worldly distinction has always been and always will be at the expense of his spiritual and moral growth; and will never give him the grasp of a living faith, nor fit him to reflect the image of the Creator.

A groveling, slavish, unsatisfied life is neither the creature of Eden, nor condition of the new earth. And the "Prince of the Kings of the Kings of the earth" cannot impart and develop in man his own perfect manhood and leave him the defenceless prey of a remourseless greed; nor the unprotected victim of the combined schemes of all the powers of darkness. No, reader, he instituted in his Kingdom that which made his blessings temporal and spiritual the heirloom of all his subjects.

We close this lecture with one more reference to that event which was to be heralded as the good news to all nations, and to every creature. And find the record of that Pentecost A. D. 33, that the will of God, as revealed by His Son had been fully honored by the holy Spirit under the authority of the heir to the throne of the universe. And the writer has no lingering doubt left as to what the sceptre of the Christ demands.

It demands the open confession that he is Lord and Christ; it demands repentence of sin, renunciation of former life with all its individual monopoly of earth's blessings. It demands the putting off the old life and the putting on of the new, by being buried and raised with him in baptism. It demands cooperation and unity of life and purpose that would entitle its living subjects to the gifts of the Holy Ghost.

The author has been much perplexed in trying to reconcile the teachings of Christ. The promise in the commission to the apostles that he would be with them always to the end of the age, the conditions existing in his kingdom at its founding, and the solution given to these things by modern thought and practice. And he now fully believes that modern reformers and church builders, who have professed to go back to Jerusalem for their model, did not remain there long enough to get the divine model so fully engraven on their hearts and minds as to reproduce it in its completeness and purity. The author disclaims any desire for honor in this regard, but he deplores the suffering of a groaning creation and is seeking for the sceptre that can dispel its foes.

The Bitter and the Sweet.

LECTURE FOURTH.

"And I took the little book out of the angel's hand and ate it up; and it was in my mouth sweet as honey; and as soon as I had eaten it, my belly was bitter." Rev. 10:10.

"And he said unto one, rise and measure the temple of God, and them that worship therein; but the court that is without leave out and measure it not, for it is given to the Gentiles and the holy city shall they tread under foot forty and two months." Rev. 11:1-2.

Nothing can be more bitter to man's selfish carnal nature, than the complete reception of God's plan as revealed in the open book.

Nothing is so hard for man to get rid of as his idolatrous love of the world and himself.

If he lives in an age of world worship and world service, for gain and human glory, the uprooting and removal of that love and worship, will constitute the bitterest cross of his whole life and being.

This change in the attitude human nature must assume toward the kingdom of heaven, indicates clearly why Christ placed so much emphacisis on this cross, the subjects of His kingdom would have to take up and bear.

Men are of necessity, each an individual part of the system, social, civil and religious, of the age and generation in which they live, therefore it was impossible to build a new institution, absolutely pure and perfect, of which Christ was founder and head, without completely changing man's relation from the old to the new.

Hence in his plan it is not the willingness to give up some things, which are the ground of this love of self, of gain and carnal pleasure, but the actual giving up that which fits man for his kingdom and to receive its blessings. Under the present standard of the church the bitterness of this cross has disappeared, and man goes on from his public profession to live in the church and serve self and the world.

All the bitterness of the worlds experience comes from the need of a perfect righteousness in the earth, and while it has rushed on from one expedient to another leaving blight and desolation in its wake, the astounding fact confronts us that the rock of the ages was planted in the earth nineteen centuries ago and its perfect fitness as a foundation for salvation, righteousness, rest and peace fully disclosed.

In order to give an enlightened age undeniable testimony as to its relation to the age of the world, in its corresponding relation to the approaching triumph of the kingdom of Christ the revelator must eat the open book; and prophesy again before many nations, peoples and tongues.

Manism and devilism combined has given to human kind one of the bitterest experiences in filling the measure of this prophecy the world has ever had, and the iron rule in the hand of Jesus so clearly pictured in triumph, gives to individual and national hope, a foretaste of infinite and eternal sweetness.

The testimony of Jesus is the spirit of prophecy, hence the revelator must rise and measure the temple (dwelling place of God.) The court (Gentile rule) could not be included and forecast in prophecy as a part of God's building because a perfect history of manism and devilism combined, whose reign has constituted the anti-Christ of past and present history, and has and is baptising the world in blood and suffering must be measured separately in the prophecy.

From the advent of the kingdom of Christ A. D 33, its authority witnessed; its righteousness revealed and established by the Holy Spirit and its authority promulgated, all other opposing powers and forces that foster corruption in the earth, must from the standpoint of reason and prophecy, of necessity be regarded anti-Christ.

Christ's kingdom, from the very nature of its great and Godlike purpose and work, admits of no rival perversion or mixture. To intercept its glorious and eternal purpose and plan on the part of man is eternal murder, and must and will shut us all from the Eternal City and the Tree of Life. To confess Christ and continue in our work to be an opposer and rival of man, make us the enemy, if not directly, indirectly, of his safety and salvation.

The selfrighteousness, conceit and vanity of this age may prevent our return to Jerusalem and taking the completed righteousness prescribed by the completed work of Father, Son and Holy Spirit, but will not prevent the question at the approaching marriage: How camest thou without the wedding garment?

Our limit will not allow us to scan the historical record of the use the two witnesses (Old and New Testaments) have made of the power given them to smite the earth with plague, but we call attention to the fact that since this enlightened age fails to find a source or a cause for the ravages made by plague, drouth, famine, pestilence, fire, tempest and storm, that the unseen hand is writing upon the wall of our bold defiance the "mene tekel upharsin" of His eternal plan and that in them the wine of His wrath will be poured out without mixture.

Just at the instance of this writing the author picked up in a neighboring town a secular paper (Inter Ocean) recording the fact that the waters of the Atlantic ocean presented all the appearance of the repetition of the plague of Egypt; that a substance that looked like blood covered the surface to the depth of eight inches and stank so it was difficult to approach the shore. That the dead animals were thrown up in winrows three feet deep around Naraganset bay, and that this condition continued for thirty days.

For proof that the New Jerusalem, the Holy City, New Heaven and the New Earth, the perfect tabernacle of God is that institution which had its advent in the literal city and temple A. D. 33, we appeal to divine testimony.

It was, under the sceptre of Christ, the blessed and glorious meeting place of God with men. The power of God in defeating unbelief, Satan, disease, sin and death, through man, was most wonderfully displayed.

It was that institution which was to be trodden under foot of the Gentiles until the time of the Gentiles were fulfilled.

Its counterfeit and enemy anti-Christ is an institution whose reign is limited to the time the true kingdom was to be trodden down.

In nothing but an institution could perfect righteousness be revealed, enforced, exemplified and rewarded.

Nothing else but a divine institution can entertain the relationship ascribed to the worshipers in the temple of God; that of children of God, saints, God's people, body of Christ, brethren, kings and priests unto God, etc.

At no other time nor place in the inspired record can we find an institution (city) in whose foundations are the names of the twelve apostles of the Lamb. Certainly their names were put into that foundation which was laid at Jerusalem A. D. 33, and they declared no other could be laid. No other institution has in it the names of the twelve tribes of the Children of Israel, and no other institution ever will be found that more effectually separated the righteous and the wicked.

God never has, nor never will save man from suffering sin and death and make him perfect except through instituted means, since perfection is a growth and the source and ground of happiness now and hereafter.

Man can never get in a happier place or state than in an institution (Tabernacle) where God dwells with him and where there is no weeping, sorrow, pain nor death and in which all these former things have passed away. When seen either in the light of reason or revelation the new Jerusalem can be nothing more or less than an institution (not a literal city) in which God dwells with man, and by His spirit cooperates with him in his recovery from sin and death, and his return to that perfection and innocence which makes man like the Creator.

Nothing but an institution can become great and fill the whole earth, and into nothing else can the kings of the earth and the nations bring their honor and glory.

History, experience and observation all prove that institutions mold and make men and the character of the civilization they build. It is rule, custom and the policies they conceive and inaugurate that bless or curse humanity.

It is equally certain that the world would be infinitely better off with an institution that created righteousness, character, spiritual mindedness, true conceptions of justice and eradicated the selfishness that inflicts only cruelty and suffering upon man.

It is significant that the eating of the open book prepares the revelator for the measurement of the New Jerusalem and the worshipers. With charity but in solemn earnestness we invite the reader to contrast this institution as it came down from God out of heaven, A. D. 33, and find now the worshipers who fill its measure.

If not, why not? Man needs salvation as much now as then. It is not right to wait until the judgment age either to be saved or to save others. Are we saved or in a position to save others when we do not fill the measure of worshipers who have constituted a part of the tabernacle of the living God and who have been measured and accepted of Him?

Every stone admitted to God's building on its foundation was measured and dare, will we, refuse to apply that measure to ourselves, our lives and works? If we do we may expect to hear him say; "I never knew you. Depart."

God help the author to fill the measure of his responsibility just here. The astounding fact confronts us that all these property rights so much sought after and worshipped by this age and generation, their entire title has descended to us from anti-Christ, and in its use we are maintaining institutions which we must admit are an offence to God and a curse to man. Why not surrender these rights and acquire title under Christ? Sooner or later it must be done and we become joint heirs with

Him. This measure is the needle's eye of His kingdom and He never has nor never will enlarge it, to admit you or me. Will we hold them as filling the measure of our hearts and lives now, and in the time of separation be found without a place to rest the soles of our feet, and with those who are angry at the triumph of the measure of His righteousness in the earth.

This is the measure Christ filled in His birth, growth, development and perfect manhood as indicated by the seamless robe He wore to the cross. As a result of this development under the ministry of the Holy Spirit we find in Him a perfect union of the human and the divine.

His saints must of necessity divest themselves of carnal worship and service and beginning with a childlike nature grow into His likeness; which cannot be done with their lives engaged in the worship and service of Mammon.

This human and divine perfection in the person of our Lord has distinguished Him and made His life conspicuous in history and in the eyes of all men; and when his professed followers cast aside their mammon worship and bring their earthly interests into joint heirship with Christ and each other, and under spiritual ministry it will distinguish the kingdom of Christ above all other institutions. It is to be presumed the Scribes and Pharisees were very good citizens, and as the world goes today, quite religious; but it takes a better righteousness than theirs to give one title in the kingdom of heaven.

The Lord understands the means of our recovery infinitely better than we, and if business push as exemplified in this decade would help to introduce one into his kingdom he never would have arrayed business push as furnishing an excuse for not entering.

His idea was if buying a piece of land, or a yoke of oxen, or even marrying a wife would become of such consequence to us that it would bar us from the great supper, it would be better to disengage us altogether from that danger and place man in such a relation to these earthly things in his kingdom that man's utter servitude to them might be obviated.

The case of Lazarus and Dives is illusurative of the truth that the lowest depth of poverty and suffering is more eligible to heirship with Abraham in God's covenant than the extreme riches of Dives, which had filled his heart and life with his portion and placed him on the wrong side of the gulf between the two extremes.

If the institution we have found providing for man's return to God and communion with him, was one of human policy and questions of dollars and cents it would be discussed on the rostrum and in the marts of trade; but the Mammon guild and Siren hope of worldly prosperity has so completely stolen and captivated the interest and admiration of the enlightened age that man will follow its receding magnet of a false hope until he is stranded amid the confusion of his own falsity.

The worst phase world worship presents is the slavery it entails, the blindness it creates, the weakness, depravity and suffering it leaves in its wake.

So long as the age continues to look amid the rubbish of its own failures for the goal of its destiny, or the fruition of its hopes, it will be left to weep at the grave that swallows its highest ambitions and to find at the end of its pursuit their emptiness and vanity. The lower the deity the smaller the worshiper.

The repeated prophecy by the revelator traces and exhibits three powers in the relation to each other as history records them down the ages.

The two witnesses in their testimony to the plan of God and its outcome.

The sceptre of Christ with its iron rule operating through his own institution, in the deliverance and salvation of men.

Anti-Christ with its counterfeit kingdoms and their corrupt systems, as seen in mystic Babylon from its rise to its fall.

The remaining space in this lecture must be given to the responsibility of the present age to the first of the three.

These two witnesses constitute God's defense against a world's complaints in the bitterness of its strife, weakness and lawlessness. The testimony they give would bring rest and peace to the troubled waters of man's unrest.

This is an age of man worship, of glory in human achievements, of exaltation in national greatness and glory.

While not insensible to the good that has been done and the advancement that has been made in many ways; we have to confess with sorrow it has brought us but little nearer the accomplishment of the great things in which God glories and the mission of Jesus made possible, than we were a hundred years ago. The world seems not to have grasped the secret of His power nor the majesty of His purpose and plan.

The bitter things pertaining to man's portion cling to him still, and under existing conditions give no clue to a way of escape. There is cruelty, enmity, passion and insensibility to suffering in man's nature yet.

There is a large place in the public heart and nature for depravity to engender degenerate schemes, and for pride and avarice to work them out even at the disregard of suffering and sacrifice of life.

Disease, plague, crime, proverty and calmity, stalk defiantly along in man's career yet, and none of the world's physicians seem to have discovered a remedy or way to escape.

We need not ask pardon for assuming that there is a way of escape and a remedy or God would not reveal his restrained wrath to man for the part he takes in these things and the conditions that engender and produce them.

Since the world has tried almost every other expedient and panacea we suggest the iron rule in the sceptre of the Christ for the reconciliation of man with man.

It seems to us morally certain that whereever men disengage themselves, their influence and works from all degenerating, corrupting agencies, and devote their energies and powers exclusively to the rescue of themselves, and their fellow men, from their corrupting power, the cooperation of Christ in a work so much his own, and with those so like himself will not be wanting.

Such an opprotunity will never pass by unimproved by Him who came to seek and save that which was lost.

Whenever men are engaged in his work in a way to accomplish his purpose to save what they gain, and bring about now and hereafter the conditions that bear witness to his work, Christ will not hold in reserve his matchless power to save and bless mankind,

The world will always find Him in his own institution and with his own people and in it there is both safety and salvation.

What a rebuke it would be, to a world seeking, world loving, money grasping age if those who confess Christ brought their wealth and all their powers of service and make a complete offering of all to the exclusive use of the kingdom of Christ in a determined and aggressive struggle for the rescue of man and his abode from all that is degrading, oppressive or destructive.

Truly it would make the kingdom like a city of refuge to the weary, endangered, fainting wayfarer when stranded amid the rocks, pitfalls and snares of a corrupt world "There would be one fold and one shephard."

With the best that has been done by the state and others organized forces, it cannot be denied that the question of home, shelter, bread, sympathy and protection, constitutes the great and oppressive burden of the masses.

The cold dry charity of the state may furnish for the time food for the stomach and shelter for the body but it takes the environment of the love of Jesus to win a man from the paths of vice and to keep him from falling after he is won.

It is not Christ's method to entice lambs into his fold just to turn them out again among the wolves and we assume the only reason his servants have, was for want of a better understanding of his plan.

The revelator records the increased use of power as the vehicle of divine wrath until it culminates in the great and decisive contest between the divine sceptre and the corrupt power it confronts.

Both the elders and saints give thanks that God reigns, that the nations are angry and for the destruction of them that destroyed the earth.

If both the churches and the world are in the right relation to God and to each other we can hardly see the need of this constant and increasing visitation of wrath, for both in that event might hope and pray that it might cease.

If an enlightened age could foresee what was demanded and enforced by such visitations and accede to the demand it would remove their neccessity of a forced compliance and the punishment it involves, and since righteousness has been revealed and exemplified in the earth, unrighteousness can neither demand nor expect toleration.

An overwhelming responsibility rests upon the builders of this generation to restore that institution which contains the only exemplification of a perfect righteousness for man the world has ever had by building again the building of God, made without hands and eternal in the heavens. It is the demand of God through the Spirit and the application of the mission of Jesus to a groaning, suffering creation.

When the world has its history written aforetime, and the events that make up its career chronicled before they transpire, as was the fate of the Jewish nation, and this prophecy forcasts the end to which all the nations are now drifting in their indifference to the sceptre which is to rule all nations with a rod of iron, they ought to be able to read the hand writing on the wall and avert the world of suffering which must otherwise inevitably enforce the lesson the prophecy teaches.

How much better to prepare for crucial events than be overtaken by them as by a thief in the night.

How convincing the fact that every day's calamitous events are a gracious reminder that the divine sceptre is held out to us, calling us to take refuge under the rocks of ages. The men or nations who love the fabrics of their own building and the carnal glory they bring them, better than they love the eternal structure of the perfect Christ with the eternal happiness and safety it affords earth's millions, will not do for pillars in the temple of our Lord, nor for kings and priests unto God in the new earth.

The world ripens fast and events culminate quickly when prophetic light is focused upon the career of nations and the character of their policies, systems and institutions.

The harvest of the earth will ripen quickly after the sowing is done, and just as surely as righteousness has been revealed as the true foundation of all social, religious and political systems, so sure will systems not founded upon the eternal principle of the fatherhood of God and the brotherhood of man through the mediation of Christ be swept away, and the "Kingdoms of this world become the kingdoms of our Lord and His Christ, and He shall reign forever and forever. (ages on ages.)

The optimism of the present can scarcely discern through the dense fog of conflicting policy, clashing faith and bewildering thought, the cubic beauty of the divine institution that once brought man into perfect fellowship with God and with each other, but after its Gentile treading is ended its glory will be brighter and its rest sweeter.

Satan in the Earth.

LECTURE FIFTH.

"And the great dragon was cast out, that old serpent called the Devil and Satan, which deceiveth the whole world, was cast out into the earth and his angels were cast out with him."

In the beginning of this our fifth lecture, we call attention to the wonder John saw in heaven, contained in this twelfth chapter. It introduces the man child who was to rule all nations with a rod of iron. John sees this child caught up to God and throne.

The woman seen represents the covenant people of God, who had been promised the sceptre of His Son. It may be said that the name woman is significant of the power of an institution to gather new subjects under its administration. When rival institutions have that power the spirit of jealousy often arouses all the energy of conquest and subjugation. This spirit animates the great red dragon, (verse 4) with seven heads and ten horns who is ready to devour this heir to the sceptre over all nations.

The inspired record justifies this description for the action of Herod in slaying innocent children shows the bloody, heartless character of the rule that was to confront the sceptre of the new born King.

From all that we know of this personality called the Devil and Satan he could not have occupied a more favorable position than to become the instigator in a corrupted, uncivilized earthly rule, and history is compelled to be true to the character of his work.

When the heir to the rule of all nations is caught up to the right hand of God, there is rejoicing in heaven, and it is declared, that now is come salvation and the kingdom of our God. That kingdom had cast him out and the only domain he had was in the earthly powers, and only for a limited time in them, his wrath is kindled and activity aroused.

Such the author understands the lesson in this part of the vision of John to teach.

The accuser of the brethren had been cast down. This locates the heaven where there is communion with God; for it was before God they had been accused. If we can find what had justified them before God, we shall find what had destroyed the accusation of Satan. Was it not the fact that thousands of Satan's former subjects had obeyed the sceptre over all nations and had become subjects of a new kingdom? Could anything else have justified them and made any accusation of disloyalty to God an impeachment of Satan?

No, there is no other logical conclusion but what Satan had been cast out of that kingdom that was to become the inheritance of all nations by the iron rule of the man child; and that iron rule would drive Satan out of that kingdom any time.

While the power of the red dragon is in iron teeth and his province under Satin is to persecute and destroy saints and to instigate unrighteousness in the earth; it is the province of the iron rule in the hands of Christ to save men, and nations from the Devil and his powers to destroy. Whenever we can find the iron rule in the hands of Jesus, we can find a Devil killer and a man saver, and earth redeemer.

My critic is envited to examine the work of that rule in the founding of the kingdom of Jerusalem A. D. 33 and point out the place in its work where Satan would assail it. Did you ever think that Satan did assail it at perhaps the weakest point?

We quote, "But Peter said Annamas why hath Satan filled thine heart to lie to the Holy Ghost?" Acts 5:3. And the Holy Ghost defended the iron rule then it defended the kingdom against Satan then and would it not defend it now?

We can plainly see that the iron rule would cause rejoicing now. That rule in the administration of the holy spirit is the regenerator of the earth. It would bring man back to God and God's gifts in unstinted measure to man. It would bring the tabernacle (dwelling place) of God to man.

One glance at the work of the spirit through man in applying that rule. In the earth at Jerusalem, A. D. 33 is enough to convince any of the mighty resources of the ever living spirit of God.

But dear reader it must bring with its power the ever living sceptre of the blessed Christ, the law of that sceptre need not be repeated here, it cannot be changed after it was revealed and ratified by the living presence of the holy spirit and confirmed by God's two witnesses clothed in sack cloth and nothing but the deceptions of Satan could blind man to its benificience and power.

We will not assume here to limit the prerogatives of the spirit of the ever living God. If it moved upon the face of the waters and brought light out of darkness in the creation it, can drive darkness and disorder out of the earth and renew it, but the love of God restrains it from doing that and leave man to the destruction of Satan.

It might be helpful to enumerate some of the benefits that would exist in contrast with the present order with the iron rule of the sceptre under the administration of the spirit.

It would wonderfully enlighten man by placing before all men the same standard of loyalty. If the gifts of God were enjoyed in the kingdom of His Son, it would convict the world of sin for not believing in him, and sweep away all misconceptions of the way of salvation. It would bring all believers in Christ into the one foundation and establish their unity upon it, and thus draw a visible line between the world and the kingdom of Christ.

It would bring mankind literally into the kingdom of Christ and disengage him entirely and practically from any allegiance or service to Satan and give man access to Christ, soul and body for healing and renewing and life giving.

This is the chief glory of the sceptre of Christ; that while sin abounds in the world and its institutions are all tarnished and leavened with evil that sceptre completely emancipates man and his life work from any affiliation with that which is corrupting or defiling

It does this by bringing under its spiritual jurisdiction the domain, products, industries and enterprises of the earth, and enables its subjects to perform all this service in His name. Unless it did this it would not be complete nor be the sceptre for all nations and for all time, and could not reinstate righteousness in the earth.

It is a glaring incongruity when a believer is left to pay tribute to the kingdom heaven and to the liquor power and do both in the name of Christ. The sceptre of Christ would bring together into cooperative bodies the scattered bewildered people of God, and as they were at Jerusalem they would all be with one accord in one place, ready to grow into an "holy temple in the Lord," and be purified unto Christ a peculiar people zealous of good works, and the work of gathering together into him all things which are in heaven and in earth would be going on. The spiritual wisdom, activity and enterprise would crown it with glory and honor and the perfect justice it administered would make the sceptre a royal diadem in the hands of our God. Under God it could pave the streets of the New Jerusalem with gold, and dry the tears from the faces of its subjects.

When God is with man there is nothing too great or too good for man to do. With man alienated from God by "wicked works" and left to the instigation of the Devil, there is nothing mean that he may not be led to do.

When the sceptre of Christ has been planted in the earth, and the foundation of the new heaven and the new earth has been laid, and the work of building upon began, when Satan and his angels (messengers) have been cast out into the (old) earth, he knows that his power has been broken, and that his time is now limited, and his wrath is kindled. The new kingdom has not yet succeeded to universal empire, but its sceptre is in the hands of a conqueror, and the spirit of the ever living God with it and its triumph assured.

If Satan can instigate human rule to assert itself in defiance of its power and authority, and deceive the nations with regard to it, it will give vent to his anger and display his wrath.

Human rule must exhibit its worst as well as its best character, in order to convince all grades of human intelligences that the sceptre of Jesus like himself is perfect.

It might be noted here that the kingdom of Christ has earned the distinction of mother, as the New Jerusalem "has become the mother of us all," as Paul testifies. In her conflict she must go into obscurity because man is carried farther and farther into darkness by the red dragon, and whose children must be killed with death and tried by the fire of Satan's wrath. Yet death cannot prevail against the sceptre of the King, for he holds the key of death and the two witnesses have faithfully recorded the laws of his kingdom, and recorded the loyal services of his subjects.

Nothing is lost that interscepts its final conquest in the earth, and soon the King will confront the world powers bringing with him a mighty host on whom the second death has no power, and fully prepared to be kings and priests unto God and reign with him.

"And the serpent cast out of his mouth water as a flood after the woman that he might cause her to be carried away with the flood, and the earth helped the woman and opened her mouth and swallowed up the flood." Rev. 12: 15-16.

False teaching, false standards, false light, and a spurious ecclesiastical order could find no other prosperous domain than man, under the delusions of a false rule, and without communion with God and the light of his spirit and counsel, man is left a prey to all forms of deception and any ism that self installed leaders might impose for their exaltation. The earth has always been hungry for both dominion and religion, and has failed to grasp the vital truth that restoration to harmony and communion with God must be the end and aim of all rule and religion, and for that reason the world has devoured and entertained vastly more of falcity than truth.

A moment's reflection ought to convince us that man cannot live in the earth and develop perfect spiritual life under a rule that compels him to bow to a carnal standard. The scriptures enjoin upon the followers of Christ obedience to the civil rule under which they live, but provides that the things in which they have fellowship and are responsible for, shall be under the law of Christ, and gives them the promise of rulership under him when he shall have put down all rule in the earth opposed to his kingdom.

It is the rule and order in the kingdom and not out of it that elevates and refines its subjects. A civilization in the earth out of harmony with the divine nature cannot continue, and never was and never can be any part of the kingdom of Christ, and we modern builders might as well take a lesson here and cease trying to put the new wine of Christ's kingdom into old bottles; the old bottles will break ere long, and while the new wine may be gathered into new bottles, the labor of putting it in the old is lost.

If the subjects of Christ's kingdom cannot build up a new civilization upon a divine basis it shows conclusively that they are as yet only half new creatures. With them "all the old things" have not yet passed away. It shows that we have not yet enough of the wisdom of God to be builders on a divine foundation under Christ.

It might be easier to build a new Jerusalem than to renew, reform or reconstruct Chicago, New York, London or Rome. Some people think that when Rome is demolished the millenium will be here; but the writer suggests that the horns will have to be knocked off the other corrupt systems before the Lamb of God can affiliate with them in the new earth.

If we recognize the fact that his divine power has given unto us all things that pertain to life and gladness through the knowledge of Christ we might be able to build a civilization on the seven fold basis of faith, knowledge, temperance, patience, goodliness, brotherly kindness and love. 2nd Peter 3:3-7.

A civilization that does not shut out the things that destroy these graces in man, is not the civilization of the kingdom of Christ, and does not enable its subjects to escape the corruption that is in the world through lust. If we want to know what constitutes a complete order of civilization, we have it here, and it is a poor kingdom that does not furnish and a bad kingdom that introduces the things that destroys it.

If the earth has opened its mouth to swallow the flood of corruption that the serpent cast out of his mouth, on purpose to carry away the kingdom of Christ, and the kingdom had to take refuge in the wilderness of obscurity to escape his flood, as God's creation took refuge in Noah's ark, the professed friends of Christ and enslaved humanity ought to bring it out of its obscurity and show its beauty and perfection.

Gold seemed to be a symbol of incorruption or of the divine nature. It is a metal that will not tarnish. Christ had such a nature, though he inherited all the weaknesses of our own; but he overcame those weaknesses by strict obedience to the will of God and by filling the measure of His work.

Neither in His own life nor in the lives of His deciples do we find any affiliation with false systems, but he commanded them to do not after their works. The kingdom of Christ has to be a kingdom within or under a kingdom in its conquest.

But for some reason the perfection of its order, the divine simplicity and import of its ordinances, the grandeur of its unity, the object of its temples of knowledge and the use it makes of the two witnesses, are more instruments of unbelief in the eyes of individuals and nations, than of faith. If we have any salt left in us, is it not time to rise up and enquire, why?

With a blush the author looks at the missions of centuries, at the armament of nations, at the domination of wealth, at the boldness and insolence of corrupting agencies, at the sword against sword, at the grinding poverty, at the dominance of pride and passion, and the mockery of human ambition and its glee of triumph, and then at the lowly Jesus beneath man's woe, and looks at the friends of Jesus and ask; Where is the sceptre in the hands of the spirit?

Will we, dare we leave that sceptre of might, of purity, of unity, of brotherly love, that glorious instrument of a divine cooperation in saving men, to rest under the corruption of Satan's flood? Or will we lift it out and rally round it with our lives, our fortunes, our powers; our hearts thrilled with the love of Jesus, our hand underneath our brother's load, and invite our once suffering King again by His spirit to walk in the midst of the seven golden candlesticks?

Within the limit of these lectures the author cannot anticipate and answer all the criticisms that his position may justly merit, but a brief space in this one will be devoted to answering one, that if nothing else bias will provoke against it, vis: That it is revolutionary and incites insurection against civil rule and the institutions they foster.

If that criticism be just, both Jews and Gentiles could not be censured for condemning the Nazerene, for he prolaimed openly the principles which the writer has found his sceptre to enforce.

No believing reverent mind will deny the sovreignty of the ever living spirit of God. Who has a right to deny anything to God that will contribute to the regeneration of all nations and races of men? Such philanthropy is worthy the right of way, and that the streets through which it marches should be paved with gold.

We ought to be willing to accord as much right to him who can restore the withered limb and unlock the tomb, abolish death and wipe the tears from all eyes, as we do to a railroad corporation, or the combination that enriches itself through the liquor traffic.

We would suggest that it would be far wiser, more just, more philanthropic to turn over the vast increase in knowledge seen in the inventions of this nineteenth century to the sceptre that brings the tabernacle of God to man, than for them to remain the mere gratification of human ambition, but the order and blessings of Christ's kingdom are never forced upon anyone and especially those who love unrighteousness and earthly glory, more than they love Christ or their fellow man. It is to his people Jesus looks for fellow helpers, and cooperation, both with himself and with each other, and the blessed spirit. Who will attempt to say he has it, and if not, why not?

The author will conclude this lecture by introducing testimony positively identifying the kingdom and its conditions after it comes from its obscurity, and with a tearful eye and prayer to God, gives utterance to the most intense desire of his heart, that his own beloved land might lead the nations in reinstating the sceptre.

"For behold I create new heavens and a new earth, and the former shall not be remembered nor come into mind. But be ye glad and rejoice in that which I create, For behold I create Jerusalem a rejoicing and her people a joy.

"And I will rejoice in Jerusalem and joy in my people, and the voice of weeping shall be no more heard in her, nor the voice of crying.

"There shall be no more thence an infant of days nor an old man that hath not filled his days.

"For the child shall die an hundred years old, but the sinner being an hundred years old shall be accursed.

"And they shall build houses and inhabit them, and they shall plant vinyards and eat the fruit of them. "They shall not build and another inhabit. They shall not plant and another eat, for as the days of a tree are the days of my people, and mine elect shall long enjoy the work of their hands.

"They shall not labor in vain, nor bring forth for trouble, for they are the seed of the blessed of the Lord and their offspring with them. And it shall come to pass, that before they call I will answer, and while they are yet speaking I will hear.

"The wolf and the lamb shall feed together, and the lion shall eat straw like the bullock, and dust shall be the serpents meat. They shall not hurt nor destroy in all my holy mountain saith the Lord." Isiah, 65, 17-25.

That the prophet Isiah pictures the new Jerusalem when the sword of persecution has passed by, and the waters of deception have receeded from the perfect foundation, and communion with God has again borne fruit, we think no one can reasonably doubt.

Let us look at the prophecy. The new heaven and the new earth constitute the Jerusalem seen in the vision of the prophet. The former heavens and earth have passed from the vision, and the memory or affections of the people, the people are a pleasure to God and a joy in themselves.

The life of man has lengthened the age of youth correspondingly. The unholy strife over earthly posessions has passed away, the earth responds abundantly to mans occupency, want and weeping have ceased, peace blessed peace is in her borders. and God responds quickly to prayer.

We ask in all defference to adverse opinion. Must there not have been a foundation for this growth, development, and change in spiritual and earthly conditions? Life is on the increase, death on the retreat, calamity no longer overtakes skill and industry, contentment rests in the abode of man, justice and equity are no longer sought after and not found.

Blind eyes have been opened and deaf ears have been restored, and the traces of the curse are being ablilerated. The seven vials of wrath have been removed and hang over Babylon, the light is no longer obscure in the habitation of the just.

God's people are coming out of Babylon and escaping her plagues, and the earth is lightened with the glory of the angel that proclaims her fallen state.

Song of Victory.

LECTURE SIXTH.

"And I saw as it were a sea of glass mingled with fire: and them that had gotten the victory over the beast, and over his image, and over his mark, and over the number of his name, stand on the sea of glass, having the harps of God.

"And they sing the song of Moses the servant of God, and the song of the Lamb, saying, Great and marvelous are thy ways, thou King of saints. Who shall not fear thee O Lord, and glorify thy name? for thou art holy: for all nations shall come and worship before thee: for thy judgments are made manifest." Rev. 15:2-4.

In our study of the open book we have seen the vail of the temple rent in twain, because Jesus the high priest of our profession had made the offering once for all.

The vail between the holy place and the holy of holies is removed because men are to become priests unto God, and offer their whole or complete offering on the altar. The court outside has been united to the undivided building of God, by placing in it a simile of the death of Christ, (baptism into his death) by faith in the death and priesthood of Christ, and in penitance and confession of sin and renunciation of former life, he brings himself and his all, and lays it all on the altar of Christ's service in the new heaven and the new earth, the now everlasting and holy temple of God.

We have seen confusion reign almost supreme in court, as to what the order established in it was for, to us an indefinite period. Baptism, faith, repentance, infantile regeneration, rising in an assembly and giving your name on the church roll, have all been matters of dispute, and even church government has been the occasion of such strife among modern builders as to dot the earth all over with opposing temples of worship and education, and creating in the human mind a dense fog of confusion.

But the foundation stands sure in the record of the two witnesses. The eternal city (new heaven and new earth) have been measured and them that worship therein. And though they take on sackcloth over the confusion of Babylon and her false reign in the earth, her foundation is just as perfect, her streets just as clean, her gates just as straight, and citizens just as single minded, as when the building sprung into its cubic beauty at Jesusalem A. D. 33. If one gate were left out it dishonors its builder, and unfits it to be a perfect heaven and earth; but thank God even Gentile treading, under the instigation of Satan cannot change it.

The writer has seen the City of Washington from the top of its famous monument. Its streets are clean and its stuctures beautiful. The work done in her temples characteristic and distinguished among all the nations of the earth, but its work is imperfect. It is subject to constant change and modification.

If the rule that was inaugurated there a century ago had been a perfect rule, removing from its citizens all motive for a personal monopoly of its blessings, because it could provide abundantly for all, and the sole ambition of each had been turned to, and employed for, the physical, intellectual, moral and spiritual growth of all its people; if all that would in any way operate adversely to all these shut out of its limits; if added to this the spirit of new life pervaded the city, in the ground it occupied, in the air it breathed, decay had been arrested, inherited disease become almost invisible.

If in its citizens the power of selfcontrol had been recovered to that extent, that each individual was a new and living example of faith purity and loving kindness, the brow of manhood no longer wore the trace of care nor the frown of anger, but the eye was lustrous with the light of love and beneficence.

No uncertainty, no discord, no questioning; all was order; the very soul of praise and prayer on every tongue.

Its citizens go out to the neighboring cities with a copy of the law and order in Washington, attended by the same spirit that had been the inspiration of the new civilization there.

Would there be any thing divine and glorious in such a mission? Would it do to compare Washington and it people to a sea of glass in contrast with the other cities of the world? Would her light be like a stone, most precious? Would Washington be a new city? Would it be the wonder of the world? And if its order and conditions extended throughout the limits of the United States, would it be glorious in the eyes of all the world?

My critic may interpose that my illustration is not applicable because it is not feasible. We answer that the history of the United States with all the corruption it has fostered, is to day a revelation and a wonder the world over, and until the foundation at Jerusalem has had a like trial, no denial of its application can be entertained. If corrupt rule could attain universal empire at the instigation of Satan, work as much desolation as it did in Twelve Hundred and Sixty years. Who would dare to measure or limit the sceptre of the ever living Christ, even for the period of One Hundred years?

But to aid us in the study of the vision of John, we now change our standpoint of observation, and inquire from God's standpoint. What would be his view of the relation. New York (or any other city) sustained to Washington?

In the latter city his love and infinite compassion is reaping its fruit and his constant blessing is resting upon it.

In the former human pride and the love of human glory is holding its millions under the iron grip of human greed and passion for gain and vain glory, in subjection to suffering, disease, corruption and death.

Would we expect the administration of an almighty soverign to be the same in character and effect in both cities? Certainly not.

The two witnesses are just as faithful in admonition and warning to New York as they are in approbation and praise to Washington.

We ask what distinguishes the people of the two cities respectively?

We answer: In Washington the people have gotten the victory over the beast, over his image, over his mark, and over the number of his name. Their experienced position and inheritance justifies the use of the harp. Faithfulness to our trust compels us to admit that in New York they remain under the dominion of them all.

The author will give his own interpretation of the beast—his image—his number—and the number of his name.

The beast represents Gentile dominion or rule, in its bitter, cruel persecution of Christianity, faith, and in the days of its greatest tyranny. The image, its modified form under Protestant influence and civilization, and his mark to represent the tribute and act of allegiance separrate organizations under that rule, have imposed upon man.

The number of his name is indicative of false authorities which in the name of man invoked man's worship and service. The mark seems to be something passing from hand to hand, as appears from the marginal reading, and appears in the connection to be a condition of life.

And when we remember that under this Gentile rule that even the very necessities of life cannot be procured, without adjusting the right to a profit upon their purchase and sale, and since the mark has in it the right to buy and sell, we know of no other interpretation that will do justice to the text. No one will deny that the pretext or plea of profit, is one of those elastic things that has in it great power to enrich and power to impoverish; to secure luxury and produce want and starvation; to lift into fame and power, and to cast down to lowest estate.

With no iron rule to restrain it, the love of gain and the power it gives proves the most exacting corrupting thing on earth. So then the happy people in Washington have escaped all liability among themselves, to persecution—to the guild of a contaminated civilization.

With numerous systems of false worship, to the insiduous corruption of covetousness and the danger that their hands will have to pay tribute to any of the manifold devices of Satan either open or secret.

Added to all this the eternal future before them is transparant as their present position like a sea of glass.

But we must not forget that this sea of glass is mingled with fire—that this fire has been cast into the earth from the golden altar—and one of the four beasts gave to seven angels seven vials full of wrath

Paul tells us that the wrath of God is revealed from heaven against all who hold the truth in unrighteousness, so we must expect unjust false rule with its multiplied false systems, all of which are now seen to be the result of the deceptions with which all the nations have been deceived, we must expect such manifestation of judgment as will undeceive them.

If the author could insert just here the calamity record of Babylom during the last forty years history of our advanced civilization, to say nothing of the threatening bold attitude of organized injustice, and its ever attendant fruit, suffering, disgrace and crime; I say just the calamity that has overtaken our struggle for advancement in civilization, it would be appaling; and when we state here that history never furnishes one case where they did occur only as a reproof and chastisement, or rebuke that they are shut out of the domain of a perfect rule by a perfect obedience, and superceded by covenant blessing only, is a truth standing omnipotent in the record of the two witnesses.

But to justify his position the author here inserts a brief and partial record in six cities in the United States, being famous fires in thirty-seven years:

Place.	Date.	Loss.
New York,	Dec. 1835,	$ 20,000,000.
New York,	Sept. 6, 1839,	10,000,000.
Pittsburg,	April, 10, 1845,	6,000,000.
St. Louis,	May 4, 1851,	11,000,000.

Portland, Me., July 4, 1866,   15,000,000.
Chicago,   Oct. 8-9, 1866, 195,000,000.
Boston,   Nov. 9, 1872,   73,000,000.

If the record is fairly proportionate; record of waste and desolation by fire, our comparison between Washington and New York is applied to the vision in the text. We cannot conceive the depth nor extent of disaster that is constantly overtaking our earth in a state of evil. Every death is an evil, every sickbed, every hospital charge, every asylum inmate, every suicide, every defalcation, every robbery, every assassination, every levy of men and means for war only helps on the work of devastation; but no claim but that of infidelity believes that it will go on forever; and since God was manifest in Christ the world is waiting for his redemption. Until all order and work in the earth, is in harmony with the divine order and work, the sea of glass is mingled with the sea of fire.

"And after these things I saw another angel come down from heaven having great power.

"And the earth was lightened with his glory; and he cried mightily with a strong voice saying; Babylon the great is fallen, and is become the habitation of devils, and the hold of every foul spirit, and a cage of every unclean and hateful bird.

"For all nations have drunk of the wine of the wrath of her fornication. And the kings of the earth have committed fornication with her, and the merchants of the earth have waxed rich through the abundance of her delicacies: And I heard a voice from heaven saying; come out of her my people that ve be not partakers of her sins and that ye receive not of her plagues for her sins have reached unto heaven and God hath remembered her iniquities." Rev. 18; 1-5.

If we could concentrate the unbiased telescope of enlightened reason, upon the corrupted, depraved and degrading side of the present system of rule and custom in the earth, it could, and would, faithfully apply to the enlightened mind, this part of the vision of John.

When we behold the highest type of manhood in state, in church, in commerce, in all departments of a proud civilization, bowing down—many under protest—to this juggernant of evil, with its mighty body of corruption eating like a canker at the vitals of purity, faith and piety,' cropping out in every movement of enterprise and in every domain of charity; it would not take long to sit in judgment upon it, and decide whether it was a fit instrument for the emancipation of man.

Mark you it is not the men, it is the instrument the rule described. It is because good people are in it and under it that the voice from heaven entreats them to come out of her.

Man has been enlightened with regard to its character, and are now informed that she is fallen out of the province of divine favor and that to get out of the range of her calamities and plagues they must come out of her.

When a ship at sea becomes so weakened by decay that she will no longer bear the strain of her machinery, and whenever she encounters a gale is liable to become a wreck, when she has all her crew at work trying to repair and buoy her; and at last when about to go to pieces from her own weakness and decay, a ship lays by massive and strong, made of material that never can decay, and fitted with machinery that never can get out of order, and weather proof construction; and the master of the noble craft says to the endangered crew: I have built this vessel specially for you come and bring all your valuable store on board, and the vessel is yours.

The longer it proudly rides the stronger it becomes. Would it not be ingratitude and insensibility to the greatest peril; to stick to the old vessel?

The history of the world shows that man cannot in his weakness construct a law or rule of life independent of devine wisdom, that will exempt from disaster nor redeem him from suffering and death: but the fact confrontes this enlightened religious age, that Jesus Christ did establish a foundation for man to build upon, that furnishes a perfect rule and a perfect order, and only enthroned corrupted human abition has trodden under foot.

The limit of this lecture will not permit the author to insert the entire chapter, but he invites the reader to read the latter part.

We call attention to the fact that the judgement is not executed upon the people, nor upon the wealth itself, but upon a city which in contrast with the New Jerusalem represents a rule or system. Hence kings, merchants, heads of commerce, shipowners combinations for gain, are the mourners at her scene of the judgement and overthrow.

The merchants weep because no man buyeth his merchandise any more. May we not reason that some order, custom, or law, has found sway and acceptance by the people that obivates, and removes their power to corrupt, and to prevent unrestrained human ambition from ascending to unsafe rule and power, as well as to make available to all the people the blessings, provided by a bountiful creator.

The city was given a name "Mystery Babylon the Great," the mother of abominations in the earth; and in profane as well as inspired history, whenever unrestrained human ambition dictated man's estate in anything, pertaing to life or its blessings, its own injustice has wrought its overthrow.

And with the sceptre of Jesus with its iron rule of complete submission to eternal equity, and benificience, of man with man, it could not stand forever and be the sceptre for all time, and for every clime.

The vision of John found in this "Mystery" the blood of all that were slain in the earth. As a woman her offspring has been billions of earth who have inherited her nature and have lived in her bondage her exactions and tyrany, have paid the wages of the sin of her service, and have gone down unto death.

With a sense of relief the author turns to a more pleasing sight in the vision of John. It is recorded in the nineteenth chapter:

"And I heard as it were the voice of a great multitude, and as the voice of many waters, and as the voice of mighty thundering, saying; Alleluia for the Lord God omnipotent reigneth." Rev. 19; 6.

That the disappearance of Babylon and the release of the people from her corruptions and exactions, should fill the earth with such rejoicing and thundering shouts of triumph, could not have been the case if the earth had not been lightened by the angel who announced her fall. But with the eyes of man open to see the cause of the corruption in her, and to see the utter uselessness of it in the light of the divine sceptre, it causes earth to rebound with rejoicing.

The eternal principle of joint heirship which existed in Father Son and Holy Spirit, in the creation of the universe and in the redemption of man, and extended to man by the sceptre of Christ, opened the eyes of so many who are under the deceptions of Babylon, who have discovered that it was enough to be a joint heir in heaven and earth with the Lord Jesus Christ, that they leave the false basis at once; and the deception Babylon has imposed on the church and the nations melts away like the dew before the sun. And while it causes great rejoicing among believers, it causes great anger among the nations, and among the opulent worshipers of the God of this world. What a delusion the custom and drift of centuries can live upon and impose on humanity.

What light is here shed upon the latter day history of the church and the world. What an era in the conquest of the kingdom of God in the earth.

The new heaven and the new earth emerge from the wilderness of obscurity. The preparation of the bride for the approaching marriage of the Lamb is rapidly going on.

She is casting off the garments colored by her long affiliation with the pomp and vanity of Babylon, to putting on their pure linen clean and white, for, the clean linen is the righteousness of the saints.

The mists of ages has cleared away uncertainty, enquiry, and doubt has given place to faith, division and strife, to unity and cooperation. wisdom, labor and enterprise are sanctified by the holy tie of a pure brotherhood, and the gifts of the blessed Spirit bear fruit in a higher, purer, stronger life.

One glance at an eror which has wonderfully mistified the study of the book of Revelation, in fact the whole bible, must close this lecture; that the earth renewed, purified, and the curse removed, was not to be the eternal abode of man. Whereas to the reverse of this prevailing idea, the scene of the entire conflict between good and evil, life and death, light and darkness, injustice and righteousness, relates to the earth as the resting place of the Tabernacle of God, and the restoration of man to uninterrupted communion with God through it.

When man has become completely invested with the divine nature which is love, such an affinity with that nature in God and in man as lifts him beyond temptation from evil. His dominion in the earth is regained, and not even the shadow of a cloud comes between man and his God.

The darkest side, the view of this problem of eviil and all its destructive consequences presents, is the fact that the great and good are alike putting all the wine of their love, faith, and prayers, into this massive mixture of discord, this mighty monster of evil Babylon, which has swallowed up the protests—the lives —the prayers—the sufferings of her millions— and exults with glee in her unholly triumph.

In the name of the risen Christ, we ask how can this unholly affiliation go on and defilement be prevented? What about the young and the weak? What about the light of the church? Is it like the light of a city set upon a hill? But light is dawning, time is passsing and Jesus lives.

The Tabernacle Restored.

LECTURE SEVEN.

"And I saw heaven opened and behold a white horse; and he that sat upon him was called faithful and true, and in righteousness doth he judge and make war. His eyes are as a flame of fire, and on his head were many crowns, and he had a name written that no man knew but he himself. He was clothed in a vesture dipped in blood, and his name is called the Word of God, and the armies which are in heaven followed him upon white horses, clothed in fine linen white and clean." Rev. 19:11-14.

When heaven opens at this point in prophecy it discloses wonderful activity.

The lease given Gentile dominion in the prophetic record has now expired and the right of universal conquest is accorded the Prince of the Kings of the earth; and the armies of heaven wait no longer.

It has never in the light of history been the plan of God to make war indiscriminately. While the world is under the dictation and deceptive influence of Babylon heaven has not a very large army in the earth, and what it has are not in a condition to make the best of soldiers; but since Babylon's false light has been extinguished and her corrupt systems brought under the ban by the light of a new kingdom, a mighty host rally under the standard of him who wears the vesture dipped in blood.

We may infer that these soldiers are clothed in seamless robes of white, constructed like the one Jesus wore to the cross, indicating that in their natures there was a perfect union of the human and divine, and that His sceptre would produce the same result in all those who were to ride upon white horses with him to the conquest.

When the seals were broken John had seen a white horse with this same rider with a single crown and with a bow going forth to conquer; but the opening of the other seals discloses horses of different colors, who in the vision represent the claims of the various achievements of the world powers by worldly policy.

The red horse the achievement of war; the black horse the achievement of commerce; the pale horse the power of persecution as a means of conquest. Rev. 6:4-8.

All these policies exhibited by world powers set aside the great and beneficient purpose and plan of a world's redeemer, and seem wholly unconscious of the fact, that they are treading under foot the one institution that can redeem and save men.

The rider upon the white horse in the vision before us, is called faithful and true, and the conquest he is making is in the interest of righteousness, justice and judgment.

He never has cast any false light upon the character of his sceptre. What it revealed as righteousness it will always demand and enforce. His own life had shed its lustre upon the righteousness he exemplified, and it robbed disease, sin and death of their power, and brought heaven and earth together in perfect reconcilliation and harmony.

But the enemy of God and man had not yet exhausted all his resources as an opposing power.

His last resort seems to have been to clothe his rule with a divided robe of respect for Christ and the Devil; to use Christ's name for a pass word and their own to wear the glory. For Babylon said: "Behold I sit a queen, and am no widow, and shall see no sorrow;" but the angel said: "As much as she has glorified herself, and lived deliciously, so much sorrow give her."

The author would courteously ask if the prophecy just quoted does not clearly describe the opulent boast of the nations today, and are they not all holding in their lustful embrace evils world wide, and age corrupting?

Does not covetousness pave the way from the humblest life to the dome of justice, and close the ear to its cry? *

That which ministers more to the carnality and depravity of man than to his recovery from both, can never be the instrument under God of man's redemption from evil

It must be an institution that changes man's relation to the law of heredity, and have that law minister to the renovation and reconstruction of the heart and mind, before the downward trend of society can be reversed.

No institution, whether church or state, that leaves man more exposed to evil in all its forms, than to good, can ever be the instrument of man's recovery and salvation. If saved, it must be in spite of them and not by or through them.

Our relation to the vision before us locates our duty on this side of Babylon's fall. God's people are in her; your children and mine are in her; her vices are staining our garments and poisoning our lives and theirs.

What is the state of our hearts toward the two sceptres? Will we stand on the sea of glass with the harps of God in our hands, or with those who stand afar off from her desolation, and cast dust on our heads while she is being consumed?

This age has produced some anomalies in the light of the apostolic record. In recent attempts to build anew on the divine foundation men have even gone back of it in their attempt to reform the church; but it seems to have escaped all these reformers that it takes both the spiritual and earthly order to constitute the true tabernacle of God. Like their predecessors their structures stand like a kind of religious leanto to Babylon, and the beauty, power and completeness of the divine model is wanting. The spiritual must include the natural in order to have the natural become spiritual.

The confusion and weakness apparent in all our modern institutions both religious and secular is due to our failure to see that in God's plan as applied by Christ there is perfect harmony, unity, and spirituality in both the spiritual and the natural or earthly order of Christ's kingdom.

If it were not so it would be impossible to unite the two natures into a perfect unity and harmony on the same foundation.

The robe of Christ's righteousness was seamlesss and woven that way from top to bottom, but the garments woven by modern systems only go halfway round us and only cover the spiritual side of our natures, and the iron rule in its application to the exposed side of human nature is lost. Spiritual life and power cannot pervade that part of life which is not under spiritual control. In visions of armies of heaven all ride horses of the same color. No other color would represent the standard borne by this army—a perfect righteousnes needs but one.

The warrior leading the armies of heaven having on his head many crowns gives assurance to a suffering misguided and misruled world of the reform of all reforms.

It will not be in the nature of a pitious appeal to the corrupt systems of men to draw back some of their deformities, and hide their beastly character out of a mock respect to the mere name of the great commander but the sword that goes out of his mouth will smite the nations with its standard of a perfect justice and righteousness.

Nothing can be more smiting in its nature and effect than the iron rule of his sceptre as a leveler and adjuster, in removing the right of a vitiated, corrupted, human ambition to monopoly of rule and possessions in the earth.

When weighed in the light of either reason or justice such right possesses neither the element of true greatness nor benificence but relegates, to the individual the right to a despotism. Such a right stands squarely across God's purpose to elevate all men alike to be kings and priests unto God in the earth and its affairs.

No man can exhibit the high and pure intent of his own will if every action of that will has to be exercised in deference to a will more vitiated and biased than his own, but if the power that controls every human will and action turns all alike to a true standard of beneficence and keeps them all turned in that direction, who dare attempt to measure man's spiritual and moral growth or the sway and extent of his united and universal beneficence?

That the standard revealed and applied by the Holy Spirit at Jerusalem, A. D. 33, established joint heirship in both spiritual and earthly blessings can neither be denied nor disproved, and until that law is restored in his kingdom in the earth, the spiritual administration must suffer for want of the cooperation of its earthly order in the advancement of His kingdom.

To the optimist the scene is inspiring. The horses of other colors with the war cry of their riders calling attention to the achievements of war, commerce, subjugation and persecution as paving the way for man's progress, are all eclipsed by the righteous splendor and heavenly purpose of the army of Jesus. How quickly the monster bubble of vain glory explodes when pierced by the perfect sword of eternal truth.

It will be humiliating indeed to the self-installed leaders, potentates and benefactors of the human race, to learn that the lowly Nazerene gave the world an institution that provided abundantly, not only for man's earthly wants, but for his recovery from sin and death, without all the sacrifice of blood, suffering and treasure the world has offered on the altar of human ambition.

All the achievements of this unbridled ambition has its vast cortege of suffering, toiling, weeping mourners to whose oppressed spirits neither progress nor victory brings relief or laurels.

It has been the comfort and the boast of the Christian workers of the present age that they could go back to that memorable Pentecost for spiritual inspiration and promise; but their eyes seem to be closed to another feature of that event just as dear to our risen Lord, as that the spirit then came in His name.

It is the fact that that spirit brought all that believed together onto one foundation. It brought their possessions and interests with them into one common joint heirship, and in them exemplified that righteoushess and fellowship, the work of Christ made possible among men.

Never before since the fall had heaven and earth witnessed such a scene, such a unity of, and such a blending together of heavenly and earthly interests. It is well to remember that the interest of the ages past and future concentrate in the city of the great King. To its shrine we go to find the cross, the tomb, the resurection and the ascension. To its shrine we must go to find the descent of the spirit, the new Jerusalem, and the employment of apostles and prophets in placing men squarely upon its new but perfect and eternal foundation.

Its advent was the culminating event of the ages, and the perfection of its work cannot be excelled by any power, human or divine.

Its sceptre brought mercy, even to the murderers of the guiltless Christ, and crowned alike the lowly and the humble, the mighty and the noble with infinite grace and peace.

It gave to dying mortals the earnest of victory over weakness, blindness, suffering and death. It was what the world needed then, what it needs now, and will have again.

The army we have seen go forth in the vision, gives assurance of world-wide victory.

The marriage of the Lamb bears witness that the bride has made herself ready and the work of regenerating the earth has been resumed, and the tabernacle of God is being enlarged.

What a privilege to be invited to the holy marriage of the perfect Christ.

What motive for a more thorough inspection of the wedding garment, its construction and the manner of putting it on.

These garments are constructed by the ministry and affect upon human nature, of that righteousness prescribed by the Holy Spirit, and which restores man to the fatherhood of God and the brotherhood of man.

It ought to be clear to us that the initial step in putting on this righteousness, would be to come squarely on to that divine foundation that provided for man's perfection in both relations.

The army seen in the vision will exhibit clearly the distinction between the divine institution with its power to restore man to righteousness and favor with God, and the world's institutions, mixed through and through with weakness, error and evil, always learning but never able to come to the knowledge of the truth. Such has always been the character of all institutions founded upon principles that admitted of a compromise between Christ and the Devil. They could never carry their full influence in favor of either and hence never are able to decide man's destiny either good or bad.

This conflict will settle forever the claims of all rival rulerships and rival systems with which the world has been blessed and cursed by the triumph of that institution that creates and enforces perfect and everlasting righteousness among men, it will solve the problem of problems, how man can become just with God, by demonstrating clearly that at the same time he must become just with his fellow man.

It is significant that the last prophetic vision of God's open book closes by condensing into one institution the elements and forces of oposing and rival counterfeit, corrupt systems, and exhibits its true character in contrast with the one perfect and eternal institution of the king of kings, and lord of lords.

This combination of opposing rival counterfeit systems, is given a name significant of its true history and character "Mystery Babylon the great," the mother of abominations in the earth.

From the mount of his observation the revelator sees clearly the ravages of blood, crime and desolation she has left in the wake of her cruel and heartless career.

If this enlightened age would study closely the light this prophecy gives, by contrasting the true nature, character, and fate, of this mystic Babylon with the righteous, glory, grandeur and eternal duration of the New Jerusalem, it might exercise a God given discretion by bringing the honor and glory of the nations out of the one into the other, but history shows the use a world loving age will make of that discretionary power is to wait until a righteous judgment sweeps away the sandy foundations of their shaky structures, and leaves their worship to weep and lament their fall.

No more vivid, impressive, and complete exhibition of the grouping together and righteous disclosure of corrupt systems, for their final judgement and overthrow could be given than is here portrayed for man's benefit.

No granduer more sublime or victorious vindication could be given God's plan for reinstating man in righteousness and reclaiming the earth from the curse than is given in the final triumph of that institution in which God dwells with man.

The book of Revelation would be unsuited to its place in the inspired record if it did not contain the prophetic record of the final issue of God's great plan which we find steadily and progressively unfolding through the entire bible.

It is instructive and interesting to note that the bible begins with the creation, the fall, the curse and the penalty death; and ends with the curse removed, man restored, the earth renewed, the dwelling place of God with man, the river of life flowing, and evil shut out of that institution in which man holds communion with God and the Lamb.

It is of vast importance to know to which of these great terminal decisive events this age with its systems and civilization stands most clearly responsible and accountable. Most assuredly the final and decisive contest of the great plan may force upon any generation the decisive and overwhelming judgments that will bring God's people out of Babylon and carry with her all her corruptions into that abyss to which this last prophecy consigns her.

The economy of God's plan as revealed in this prophecy exhibits Babylon's fall and overthrow as occuring on this side of the first resurrection and the marriage of the Lamb.

In order to enlist in the armies of heaven, God's people must come out of her; there is no other way of escape from her sins and her plagues.

In order to show conclusively that the present systems belong to Babylon, we must recur to the opening of the seals as recorded in chapter six,

At the opening of the first seal John saw a white horse, and he that sat on him had a bow, and a crown was given him and he went forth to conquer; which shows Christ with his sceptre of righteousness confronting corrupt systems.

The opening of the second seal reveals a red horse, and the mission was to take peace from the earth, and to instigate war.

The opening of the third seal reveals a black horse, whose rider has a pair of balances in his hand, and a voice was heard in the midst of the four beasts; a measure of wheat for a penny and see thou hurt not the oil and wine.

The opening of the fourth seal sends forth a pale horse and the name of his rider was death; death and hell followed him—all the world knows his cruel reign of persecution.

We have here arrayed in opposition to the white horse and his rider, three other policies or systems that would command the allegiance and service of men, and in their nature and extent be rivals of the divine sceptre.

The war policy as a means of conquest, which even now claims recognition as a missionary force.

The commercial policy as an achievement of greed for gain, pride and indulgence in luxury. Its prophetic cry is being repeated today—hurt not the oil and the wine even if they could claim as many victims as war and persecution combined, to our commerce—they are a necessity in our civilization. They cannot be hurt without infringing upon our rights and taking away our liberties.

It does not seem possible that men can be soldiers under any of these colors and at the same time wear a uniform composed of seamless robes of white and ride upon white horses with Christ to conquest.

The policy of the kingdom of Christ is a clean unmixed policy and its war cry is the restoration of a perfect righteousness in the earth, and all who pray "Thy kingdom come" should lose no time in renouncing their responsibility for the mixed and misleading policies of this mystic Babylon, and by coming under the perfect righteousness of the sceptre of Christ take the seamless robe of white worn by the armies of heaven. As an overwhelming argument in favor of speedily coming out we suggest the fact, that in this bold and faithful prophecy, Babylon, the mother of abominations in the earth, goes out of sight in the abyss, while the kingdom of Christ reign forever. (ages on ages.)

God grant this little book, imperfect as it may be, may in a small degree fill the mission of the angel who lightened the earth with his glory, and who cried mightily with a strong voice; "Babylon is fallen, come out of her my people that ye be not partakers of her sins and that ye receive not of her plagues."

A brief glimpse at the glorious institution we have tried to trace from its advent A. D. 33, to its triumph, must close this our seventh and last lecture.

In Rev. 21:9, the angel introduces it to the vision of John as the bride, the Lamb's wife. It is instructive to study the family record, for it is the record of the great family of God "who were born not of the blood, nor the will of the flesh, but of God."

This great family throng make up that glorious institntion against which the gates of death opened so wide by the beastly opposition could not prevail. Thank God, the nations of them that are saved walk in the light of it and the kings of the earth bring their honor and glory into it.

It needs no temple, for the Lord God and the Lamb are the temple of it.

In its twelve foundations are the names of the twelve apostles of the Lamb slain from the foundation of the world.

In its gates are the names of the twelve tribes of the Children of Israel. Through the twelve tribes the gates of God's eternal plan opened to all Israel and to all nations. Through the twelve apostles were laid its twelve foundations for all nations and for all time.

From the throne of God and the Lamb within it, flows the river of life, with the tree of life on either side, bearing their twelve manner of fruits.

The tree of life on either side of the river are fit emblems of the two Olive trees standing before the God of all the earth called God's two witnesses, containing the bread of life, and from between their two dispensations at Jerusalem, A. D. 33, flows the blessed dispensation of the Holy Spirit which becomes the water of life to all who will take of it freely.

This divine institution is God's eternal plan, revealed to man by His word, executed by Christ and applied to man by the Holy Spirit. It contains provisions for bringing before the bar of Christ's perfect judgment all men and all nations.

The perfect standard of His sceptre must, and will, be accepted or rejected by every human being. Neither Satan, sin nor death prevents the mediation of the perfect Christ from settling every man's personal account with the Creator.

The two resurrections as exemplified at the first advent, the first at the resurrection of Christ when many of the saints arose and appeared to many in the city, and the general resurrection as pefigured in the resurrection of Lazarus, the widow's son, and many other cases, at least by inference, are proof positive that the great executive of God's plan holds the key to both man's present and future existence, and that sooner or later all must come under

His sceptre or incur the penalty of the second death.

This last prophetic description of God's institution shows vividly its power to separate good from evil, truth from error, and the righteous from the wicked, and is proof positive that it will fulfill its mission and the separation take place.

A forced separation is what God deplores, and what man should avoid. The world should learn wisdom both from its age and from prophecy. Upon us now rests a responsibility as high as heaven and as broad and great as the welfare of this generation in which we live, to heed God's prophetic voice of warning and quickly reinstate the sceptre of Jesus.

The rival attitude of the world powers now makes one prophecy at least suggestive that its fulfillment might precipitate the world into trouble and confusion world wide and heart rending. It reads; "And one of the four beasts gave unto the seven angels seven golden vials of the wrath of God that liveth forever and forever." Rev. 25:7. National rivalry is a poor foundation for rest.

As we have found the divine institution, there is a wide distinction between that within and that which is without, and without this distinction it could not exist in its perfection, its power and its glory.

The two classes most vitally interested and affected are both present to witness the affect of the separation of one class from the other, which is necessary in order to the safety of those within, and to place them in a right position to influence those outside to abandon that which shuts them out.

Those without do not have even a representative voice in regulating the affairs within this happy and righteous institution, and even money could not procure such a privilege. No doubt Satan would rejoice if it would admit both him and his angels; and no doubt those within are equally happy that neither can gain any access to their pure and holy fellowship.

In Rev. 13:6-8 and in 17:12-14 the prophecy carries the institution founded at Jerusalem. A. D. 33, into subjugation by the world powers at the instigation of Satan, and out of its apparent defeat to its final triumph and glory under Christ.

Its identity at its founding and at its triumph is as clear as prophecy could make it. Its being called "the New Jerusalem" connects its advent, intervening history, and triumph with the typical city of the great King.

In both its advent and in its triumph the Spirit and the Bride say come—and whosoever would might take of the water of life freely. Its streets were paved with the gold of its divine nature, and those who walked them inherited its divine purity and power.

Those who obeyed its commandments, entered its gates and partook of its tree of life, and drank of its great river of life.

The leaves of its two Olive trees on either side are ample enough for the healing of all the nations and its foundations broad enough to receive all their honor and glory.

May the graphic picture given it by the last of God's prophets, impress the hearts of all the readers of this little book with the inevitable conclusions to be drawn from its advent, history and triumph.

It is God's holy institution in which he meets and dwells eternally with man.

In it there is salvation from wrath—the curse—from Satan—sin and the second death. Out of it there is not a shadow of a promise of sa' ation from either.

God has placed at the option of men and nations to build on its eternal indestructable foundation or upon the sand of humanism and world worship.

Joyfully would the author meet those who like Simeon of old are waiting for the kingdom of God; but until he can find upon the earth its pure holy and single hearted fellowship must live in the consciousness that he walks the streets of this mystic Babylon a pilgrim and a stranger in the earth.

Note.

All who, after reading this volumn, feel that Christ would be honored, and the world be blessed by the restoration of his own institution as founded by His appostles are invited to give their name, address and any suggestion they wish to make on a card, addressed to Armour, South Dakota.

E. R. ALLYN,
Author.

www.ingramcontent.com/pod-product-compliance
Lightning Source LLC
Chambersburg PA
CBHW022129160426
43197CB00009B/1211